PRAISE FOR *RIDICULOUS FAITH*

"Francis and I have personally witnessed the radical (Ridiculous) change in Shelene as she has stepped out in faith time and time again. We believe you should err on the side of action; and Shelene will encourage you to do just that."

> —Lisa Chan, bestselling coauthor with
> husband Francis Chan of *You and Me*
> *Forever*

"Need encouragement? Read *Ridiculous Faith*. It'll help you remember all things are possible with God!"

> —Karen Kingsbury, #1 *New York Times*
> bestselling novelist

"Want to infuse your faith with supernatural inspiration? You've found a book for doing just that—and it will change your life!"

> —Drs. Les and Leslie Parrott, authors of
> *Saving Your Marriage Before It Starts*

"I'm not sure I've met a leader in the past few years who embodies faith in action like Shelene Bryan. Her fire for doing something for God is contagious and I believe she is one of the best voices to write about faith. I can't wait for people to read this inspiring work from an inspiring friend!"

> —Tyler Reagin, executive director of
> Catalyst

"If you are in a season of needing a miracle, you will find strength and hope from the beautiful promises and miracles revealed in Shelene's book."

> —Cindy Monroe, founder, president, and
> CEO of Thirty-One Gifts

"Shelene Bryan is one of my favorite people on the planet. Her ability to both challenge and encourage, while making you LOL right after bawling your eyes out, is a true gift. Can't wait for you to experience her take on our ridiculously good God!! Read this book!"

—Brad Lomenick, former president of
Catalyst; author of *H3 Leadership* and
The Catalyst Leader

"In a time when our fears threaten to eclipse our faith, my friend Shelene Bryan takes us on a faith-building journey that leaves us confident in an unbelievably good God."

—Lani Netter, producer of *The Shack*

"Shelene's sheer energy and joy for life is ridiculously captivating in every good sense of the word! I find it fascinating as a cognitive neuroscientist and Christian to see how Shelene uses her mind to believe God's Word and to change her life and the lives of all she can touch!"

—Dr. Caroline Leaf, cognitive
neuroscientist and communication
pathologist, author, and TV show host
of *Switch on Your Brain*

"*Ridiculous Faith* will challenge you to stop treating God as a means to an end but to discover who he really is as the end we're each longing for. "

—Joshua Straub, Ph.D., author of *Safe
House: How Emotional Safety Is the
Key to Raising Kids Who Live, Love,
and Lead Well*

"This book will rock your world! Shelene is the real deal and this book will change your life and strengthen your faith and your relationship with Christ."

—Laura Pettitte, wife of New York
Yankees retired pitcher Andy Pettitte

RIDICULOUS FAITH

Experience *the* Power *of an* Absurdly,
Unbelievably Good God

SHELENE BRYAN

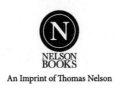

NELSON
BOOKS

An Imprint of Thomas Nelson

Published in Nashville, Tennessee, by Nelson Books, an imprint of Thomas Nelson. Nelson Books and Thomas Nelson are registered trademarks of HarperCollins Christian Publishing, Inc.

The author is represented by the literary agency of Alive Communications, Inc., 7680 Goddard Street, Suite 200, Colorado Springs, Colorado 80920, www .alivecommunications.com.

Thomas Nelson titles may be purchased in bulk for educational, business, fund-raising, or sales promotional use. For information, please e-mail SpecialMarkets@ThomasNelson.com.

In some instances, names, dates, locations, and other identifying details have been changed to protect the identities and privacy of those mentioned in this book. Stories are based on true events with the exception of chapter 8 in which the characters are fictionalized.

Library of Congress Cataloging-in-Publication Data

Names: Bryan, Shelene, 1968-
Title: Ridiculous faith: experience the power of an absurdly, unbelievably good God / Shelene Bryan.
Description: Nashville: Thomas Nelson, 2016. | Includes bibliographical references.
Identifiers: LCCN 2015036334 | ISBN 9780718021276
Subjects: LCSH: Faith.
Classification: LCC BV4637 .B827 2016 | DDC 234/.23—dc23
LC record available at http://lccn.loc.gov/2015036334

Printed in the United States of America

16 17 18 19 20 RRD 10 9 8 7 6 5 4 3 2 1

In loving memory of Katherine Anne Dickens, my hero.
Thank you for showing me what living a life for
Jesus looks like amid difficult circumstances.
I can't wait to see you again in heaven . . . forever.
July 19, 1943–December 31, 2013

Love,

CONTENTS

Foreword   ix

Ridiculous? Really?   xiii
Chapter 1 Direct Deposit   1

Part One: Going to the Mountain   9
Chapter 2 To the Mountain   11
Chapter 3 A Voice from Heaven   23

Part Two: Seeking the Face of Jesus   35
Chapter 4 A Full Car   37
Chapter 5 A Full House   49
Chapter 6 Coolio's Faith Walk   63
Chapter 7 Free to Go   75

Part Three: Finding Power in the Promise   83
Chapter 8 Hidden Promises   85
Chapter 9 Naturally Noah   95
Chapter 10 The Hands of God   105
Chapter 11 Message in a Blanket   119
Chapter 12 A Father's Ridiculous Faith   131
Chapter 13 Mountain-Sized God   139
Chapter 14 It's Only a Scratch   149

CONTENTS

Part Four: Putting Faith into Action   155

    Chapter 15 Can You Spell That?   157

    Chapter 16 The Master Bedroom   163

    Chapter 17 #Seniors Skip   173

    Chapter 18 Texas Hold 'Em   187

Part Five: Leaving a Legacy of Faith   197

    Chapter 19 First-Class Seats   199

    Chapter 20 Life Story   209

    Chapter 21 Marvelous   217

    Chapter 22 Back to the Bank   227

Acknowledgments   231

Appendix God's Promises   235

Notes   239

About the Author   241

FOREWORD

By Candace Cameron Bure

If you are holding this book, let me tell you, you are in for the ride of your life! Shelene Bryan has not only been a close friend for the last twenty-four years but has been an inspiration to me as someone I've witnessed push the boundaries of a safe faith. Since I was fifteen years old, I watched her go from a young driven career woman to a driving force after God's own heart. She has prayed me through years of my own ridiculous faith, whether in my marriage and family life, on *Dancing with the Stars*, *Fuller House*, or as cohost of *The View*. She's been such a bright light in my life and I'm proud I get to share her with you!

Shelene's personality is larger than life, commanding every room she walks into, yet she is one of the most grounded and humble women I have ever known. Her words are full of wisdom and passion because of her deeply rooted love for God and the Bible.

And her life backs it up.

As long as I've known Shelene, there has been nothing more important to her than her husband and two children. She's always lived out her family first, yet she has been passionately driven to excel in business. After finally reaching the status of successful Hollywood producer, a lightbulb went off in her faith. During a get-together with some girlfriends at her house, one woman saw the pictures of her two sponsored children through an organization called African Renewal Ministries. This woman asked Shelene how she knew if those kids were real or just a front for some guy's new Porsche. Shelene took it as a challenge and flew to Africa to find out. What she encountered there sent her on a wild, faith-filled adventure to ultimately ditch climbing the corporate Hollywood ladder and give everything she had back to the Lord. One of charities I'm most passionate about, Skip1.org, which Shelene founded, came out of that trip.

Ever since that trip, I have watched Shelene live a *ridiculous faith*. When I'm around her, one of the things I always hear her say is that our life is a vapor; that we are all just exiting here and God can call us home whenever He wants. She wakes up every day feeling the urgency of obeying God, serving Him to her fullest, and sharing His goodness with others.

The book you're holding right now contains the adventures God invited Shelene to take and the lessons He's shown her along the way. And let me be the first to say, there are some crazy adventures!

Whether your life feels overwhelming, underwhelming, or you're just coasting along, hear this! God never intended for you to live a comfortable and safe faith. He wants to take you on an adventure to show you how absurdly unbelievably good He is. But you can't be a couch potato and still witness God's miracles. He's inviting you to live a ridiculous faith.

I can't think of someone I trust more, respect more, or

will listen to more than Shelene. "Let your light shine before others, so that they may see your good works and give glory to your Father who is in heaven" (Matthew 5:16). When I read that, I think of Shelene. She is the real deal. I know because I've been watching her ridiculous faith for most of my life.

Let her adventures with God make you want your own!

RIDICULOUS? REALLY?

When I speak of "ridiculous faith," I don't mean anything that is preposterous or laughable. Far from it. I'm going by the newer sense of the word—the dictionary entry that defines *ridiculous* as "absurdly or unbelievably good."[1]

That's the kind of faith I believe God has called us to. Faith that is supernatural from start to finish. Divinely breathed faith that breaks the constraints of human belief. Dynamic faith that demolishes fear and indifference and makes it possible for us flawed, ordinary people to do God's work here in the world. Faith that does the impossible—like move mountains and transform the human heart.

Faith that is absurdly, unbelievably good because it depends on an absurdly, unbelievably good God.

This book is an invitation to join me on a journey to discover that kind of faith—an ark-building, sea-parting, lion-taming faith that leaves us all in awe of the Creator of it all. Along the way I will share some simple truths that have changed my thoughts, changed my heart, and changed my life from a self-centered, fear-driven disaster to a life of supernaturally empowered confidence. I'll also share some of my ongoing struggles because, while I have come a long way, I'm definitely not where I want to be yet. Sometimes I feel I'm just getting started. But I'm not really worried about that, because I know by that God still has me.

So are you in? Are you ready to experience something absurdly, unbelievably good?

one

DIRECT DEPOSIT

And without faith it is impossible to please
God, because anyone who comes to him must
believe that he exists and that he rewards those
who earnestly seek him.
—Hebrews 11:6

It was early December in Southern California, and while many parts of the country were dealing with rain, snow, and generally miserable weather as the Christmas season approached, all Los Angeles was enjoying its usual preholiday winter weather—that is, no winter at all. It was seventy-five degrees, and not a single cloud could be seen from the open sunroof of my shiny black sports car. On the passenger seat next to me rested a small blue bank-deposit bag containing a few checks, a large amount of cash, and the deposit slip I had dutifully filled out a few minutes earlier while sitting in my office at my talent management company. It was my lunch hour, and I relished the chance to get out of the hustle of the Hollywood scene for even a few minutes. The sun felt amazing on my face as I drove down Ventura Boulevard toward the bank. After negotiating my way through the parking lot jungle, I slid into an empty parking space.

As I entered the bank lobby, I realized everyone in the free world seemed to have had the same idea. So much for a quick lunchtime deposit. I stood in a line with about ten people in front of me, and it was filling up fast behind me.

Then I met Mrs. Impatient. A pretty fifty-something woman dressed to the nines in an impeccably tailored suit and expensive heels, she rushed into the bank in a whirlwind of self-importance. From the look of her jewelry, she was not shy about flaunting her wealth. A rock the size of Gibraltar adorned her left hand. She was not exactly subtle when she stepped up behind me in line and began to complain loudly to no one in particular, "Oh my. We will be in this line for an hour. Three tellers—are they serious? It's lunchtime. You would think they would be smart enough to bring on more tellers. I will never get to my lunch meeting at this pace."

"You can go in front of me," I said as graciously as I could muster, although I knew that a client would arrive at my office in about twenty minutes.

"Oh. Thanks," she murmured as she stepped into the space I had made in front of me. "Not like it's going to make that big of a difference. There are still six people ahead of you."

As the seconds ticked into long minutes, several more patrons rushed into the bank, only to be confronted with the growing line of restless customers. The young, dark-haired guy in line behind me seemed particularly aggravated. His eyes were shifting back and forth between the tellers as if he could make their task go faster by his intense gaze.

I began to wish the bank would open a separate line for deposits as I had seen in the past. Unexpectedly, as if he could read my thoughts, a teller yelled out, "Anyone with a direct deposit?"

"*Me!* I have a deposit!" I proclaimed, waving my blue zippered bag in the air as he motioned me forward. As I made my way past the remaining three people in line, I could feel Mrs. Impatient seething with fast-pass envy while she stared daggers at my back. I greeted the deposit teller and began to unzip my deposit bag.

Suddenly a deep voice shouted, "Everybody down!"

Spinning around to see what was going on, I saw the dark-haired, fidgety guy who had been in line behind me throwing a T-shirt to the ground. The T-shirt, which I had not noticed before, had been wrapped around his hand to conceal a black semiautomatic pistol, which he now had raised to shoulder level. Amid gasps, shrieks, and screams, every person in the bank lobby hit the cold, polished floor as if a concussion wave had struck them, knocking them to their knees.

The gun menacingly swept across the room as if searching for its first victim. Suddenly the man leapt over the top of the teller counter and demanded that the tellers fill a bag he handed them.

The room went eerily silent, the shrieks of customers and commands of the robber seemed to fade away, and there I was kneeling on the floor with my hands cradling each side of my face as I leaned my forehead on the back side of the teller counter. I felt strangely alone as I began to pray silently: *Dear God, save me, help me. I don't want to die. If he does shoot me, God, please make it a clean shot. I don't want to be a burden to anyone.*

I was brought back from my thoughts by a tapping sensation on my leg.

Oh no. This is it. He's found me.

But as I peeked out from between my fingers I saw it was not the robber who had tapped me on my leg, but was Mrs. Impatient. Apparently she had been called to the teller window next to mine before the robbery began. And now, as the robber was collecting cash from each teller's drawer, we were right next to each other on our knees. She was knocking my leg with her hand, trying to get my attention.

As I looked over at her, something seemed different. Her face seemed slightly misshapen, somehow bigger. She looked at me with bulging eyes, staring at the wedding ring on my left hand and nodding as if she was trying to tell me something. I stared back in confusion, wrinkling my brow and slightly shaking my head as if to ask, "What are you saying?" She looked me right in the eyes and opened her mouth. I immediately realized why her face had seemed misshapen. Her open mouth revealed a cavern of treasure that would have made Blackbeard the pirate proud. She had stripped her gold-laden fingers clean of her rings, including the giant rock of Gibraltar, and stuffed them into her mouth.

"Yo wing," she tried to whisper, pointing to her mouth as what looked like a diamond bracelet tried to seep out the side.

"Shhhh," I whispered back, terrified that her muffled voice might attract unwanted attention. Then, seconds later, feeling bad about my scolding, I pointed at my own earlobes while nodding toward her ears.

She reached up to her ears in a panic. Her fingers closed around the unbelievably large diamond studs she had forgotten to devour. She immediately yanked them off and, incredibly, managed to successfully stuff two more rocks into her mouth.

There we sat, Mrs. Impatient and me, huddled on our knees awaiting our fate. I could hear the tellers one by one opening their cash drawers and I could hear the robber stuffing the cash deeper into his bag. Then I heard him jump back to the lobby side. As his footsteps clomped closer and closer in my direction, I pressed my body deeper and deeper into the wall.

Just blend in, Shelene. For once, just blend in—

The footsteps persisted, closer, closer—then stopped.

"And *you* with the deposit."

What? Me? Frozen in fear, I didn't move. In that split second I imagined what was going to happen next. He was going to grab me under my arm, lift me up, put the gun to my head, and say, "Open the safe, or I'll kill her!"

At that moment I cried out to the only hope I knew of. God. *Dear God, please save me. Don't let this man kill me.*

A hand reached down and scooped up the bank-deposit bag I had been clutching tightly. The bag came free from my hand. My eyes stayed closed. *Don't look at him. If you don't see him, you can't identify him. If you can't identify him, he won't need to kill you.*

Reverberating footsteps once again filled the silent room, but this time they trailed away from me and toward the front doors of the bank. As they progressively faded into the distance, we were all still frozen; no one moved a muscle in the silence. I did not dare look up.

"He's gone. You can get up now," one of the tellers announced in a shaky voice.

Could it be true? Did we survive? Thank You, God. Thank You.

I took the first breath in what seemed like minutes. Relief rolled over me like a wave.

Mrs. Impatient began disgorging her mouth of rings and jewels. As she did so one of her earrings fell and rolled along the floor. I stooped to pick it up and handed it to her. "Well, I guess now you have a good excuse to be late for lunch."

"Thanks," she replied. "I was looking for that."

CAPTURING FLICKERING FAITH

In the months that followed, the perpetrator was eventually caught, but not until he completed a string of similar robberies up and down the Highway 101 corridor from Ventura to downtown Los Angeles. Over time, I gradually recovered from the trauma of that experience, although residual anxiety would haunt me for years to come.

In the nearly twenty years since that bank robbery experience, I often have had a nagging question about how I reacted. Why is it that in moments of true desperation we instantaneously acquire faith like we have never had before?

No, it doesn't happen to everyone. Apparently Mrs. Impatient was way more concerned about her jewelry than she was about God. But it definitely happened to me. That robbery happened at a time in my life when my relationship with God was barely an afterthought, and yet my instantaneous reaction to that moment of terror was to pray. God became my *only* thought.

Even the most hardened hearts tend to look to the heavens in moments of life and death. In those instances when we feel helpless and powerless, we instinctively cry out to our Creator. There is even a term for the phenomenon: "battlefield conversion," a reference to soldiers who cry out to God when their lives are on the line. But more often than not, the changed perspective that caused us to look heavenward quickly fades and we settle back into our not-so-inspired lives. That certainly happened to me. It would be quite a few more years before I made a serious commitment to God and opened my mind and heart to a different kind of faith.

Hebrews 11:6 tells us that "without faith *it is impossible to please God*, because anyone who comes to him must believe that he exists and that he rewards those who earnestly seek him" (emphasis added). If that's true, I have always wondered, why does faith sometimes seem to disappear as fast as it came? Are we doomed to have flickering moments of faith—when we cry out to God in desperation—that later fade, leaving us powerless and ineffectual and sometimes terrified?

After years of failure and knuckleheaded trial and error, I am confident the answer is a very simple but definite no. I have learned that when we seek a true view of God's unseen faithfulness to us and get serious about claiming His amazing promises, even the tiniest seed of faith in our hearts can become an unstoppable force for love in our lives.

How to capture that tiny seed of faith is the quest that

has driven my pursuit of God and has compelled me to write these pages. His faithfulness is something I will not fully comprehend until the day He discloses it to me. Someday He may show me a little blue bank bag riddled with bullet holes that never existed because of His unseen intervention in the bank that day.

I certainly don't have all the answers. I have barely been able to put my finger on a few of these in the years that have passed since the robbery. But I do know the One who has all the answers. And not only the answers—He even knew I would be asking the questions long before I did. And for the privilege and the promise of the opportunity to get to know such a faithful God, I am grateful.

Heavenly Father, open my eyes to Your unseen faithfulness. May my view of You be deepened and expanded so that in response to who You are, I can live a life of ridiculous faith. Amen.

part one

GOING TO THE MOUNTAIN

To embrace a life of ridiculous faith, I have learned we have to go the mountain. I am talking about following the example of Moses, who in the midst of the challenging, relentless assignment of leading his people to the promised land, took forty days to go to the top of Mount Sinai to be alone with God. That experience was life altering and faith exploding. The intimacy Moses experienced on the mountain with God gave him a ridiculous faith because on that mountain Moses "saw Him who is invisible." If we want ridiculous faith, we need to find and climb our own mountains. The size and quality of our faith is directly related to how well we know God. When we get to know who He really is, we can't help but fall on our knees in awe-inspired faith.

two

TO THE MOUNTAIN

*Then Moses entered the cloud as he went on up
the mountain. And he stayed on the mountain
forty days and forty nights.*

—Exodus 24:18

The summer our son, Blake, turned thirteen, my husband,
Brice, announced he was going to take Blake on a backpacking
trip. This trip was exclusively for "men," Brice said. By turning
thirteen Blake was entering manhood, so they were going to
mark that occasion with a serious rite-of-passage trip to the
mountains.

I was thrilled about this man trip, because as difficult as
it was for Brice to take time away from the demanding task of
leading his law firm, I knew the intentional time he invested
in our son would create the bond of trust every young man
needs with his dad. I was also thrilled because I did not have
to be dragged along on another "adventure" involving sleeping

bags, tents, and bug repellant. I figured the boys could go do their "man" thing and our daughter, Brooke, and I would go shopping and get our nails done, celebrating our "girl" thing.

The boys began to make the preparations. They decided they were going to take a trail to see a place called the Great Western Divide in the southern Sierra Nevadas.

Shortly before the trip, Brice was looking over a big trail map he had spread out on our dining room table. I asked him, "Honey, do you need a guide or something? How do you know where to go or what to do?"

"Dooon't worry," he said. "I have spent weeks in the wilderness. I have this little backpack trip under control."

"But that was years ago. Are you sure you don't want to at least consult a guide?"

"If it makes you feel better, we are following the same trail the REI guides take on their group events. See this brochure?" He thrust a brochure at me with a flip of his hand. I looked through it and quickly grasped that REI is an equipment and outfitting store that does group hiking trips. While perusing the brochure, I saw he had highlighted the trail route in it.

"Are you sure you don't want to go with REI? They have professional guides to show you the way."

Brice glared at me with a look that said, "Stay out of *man* business!"

I knew not to push this any further.

"Okay," I said, "I'll leave you alone."

The next day Brice and Blake made a trip to REI to get everything they needed for their trip. Apparently they thought the living room was a great place to deposit their purchases. When I walked in, the floor was littered with their gear:

backpacks, pads, a tent, freeze-dried food, a tiny stove, ultra-light cooking pans. You would have thought they were going for a month.

"What's that?" I asked, pointing to a black plastic barrel-shaped canister.

"That? Oh, that's our bear can."

"*Bear can?*"

"Yes, a bear-proof barrel. So bears can't open it. All our food goes in there."

"You are going where there are *bears?*"

"Yes, honey, there are bears in the mountains."

"Seriously? Now I have to be worried about you guys being eaten by *bears?*"

"Actually, there haven't been any fatal bear attacks in California in decades," Brice said emphatically. "In fact, in all of North America there are only three deaths per year by bears. Whereas last year there were twenty-six deaths by dog attacks and ninety deaths by lightning strikes."

"What . . . are you a walking encyclopedia of *bear* statistics?" I asked.

"No, I just figured this would come up. Let's just say I'm prepared. And to put your mind at ease, take a look at this." He proudly held up what looked like a small fire extinguisher with a red trigger spray gun on top, still in its plastic packaging.

"What, may I ask, is *that*?"

"This is the latest in anti-bear technology, a high-powered spray-stream bear repellant. Basically it's pepper spray on crack."

"God forbid if you get close enough to a bear to hit it with that stuff," I said.

"You could call it a 'bear necessity,'" he said with a smile.

I rolled my eyes and left the boys to finish their packing.

———

The next day they woke me at 5:00 a.m. to say good-bye. Why do man trips always seem to start much earlier than normal trips?

I gave them each a kiss and said, "Please call when you get there."

"Okay. We love you!"

The following is what happened on the man trip, as it was told to me by my husband and son.

———

The road trip from Thousand Oaks, California, to the Wolverton trailhead in Sequoia National Park was uneventful except for a few made-up road-trip songs and limericks that had father and son cracking up.

By the time they arrived at the trailhead parking lot, it was 11:00 a.m. They couldn't wait to get on the trail. With loaded packs strapped to their shoulders, they bounded up the trail, which wound its way through awe-inspiring forests of ponderosa pines, douglas and white firs, and the majestic giant sequoia trees. The forests were interspersed with lovely meadows. A small stream of crystal-clear, ice-cold water ran beside the trail. On one occasion three deer stood on the path ahead, a momma and her two fawns sipping water from the stream. The deer looked up upon hearing the oncoming hikers and darted into the trees.

As the morning changed to afternoon, with five or six miles conquered and their pace slowing from the relentless ascent and the heavy packs, they came to the edge of a small hill that over-looked a giant open meadow and stopped to take in the amazing scene. The trail-side stream took its own path and tumbled its way down a small waterfall, then crossed a stunning green grass-land dotted with wildflowers. Noticing this pristine setting and seeing the trail ahead rising to another giant hill, Brice picked a nice spot on a fallen pine tree overlooking the waterfall.

"It's lunchtime," he announced as he swung his backpack off his tired shoulders.

"Sounds good, Dad."

Brice proceeded to pull out a tuna sandwich and a BLT stacked high with extra bacon. Blake pulled two PB&Js from his pack. They sat on the log with their feet dangling over the riverbed and enjoyed their feast. Brice hungrily devoured the tuna sandwich while the BLT sat on top of his open backpack, warming in the sun. The aroma of bacon filled the air. Having eaten the first sandwich, Brice got up to retrieve the BLT from the top of his pack.

As he stood up he had a full view of the meadow. Something moving caught his eye. Unsure as to what it was, he strained to get a better view. At first it looked like a large tree stump was moving across the meadow toward them. But suddenly the hair on the back of Brice's neck stood straight up. That was no stump. The biggest brown bear he had ever seen was moving at a fast clip right toward them. It was about a football field off. *The BLT!* Brice realized the sandwich with extra bacon had been sitting out in the open, upwind from the bear. *That sandwich is a homing beacon!*

"Blake," Brice said as calmly as he could. "Put your food away *now*—we've got company!"

Blake looked up from his PB&J banquet. "Wha—?" He spied the oncoming bear, and his eyes grew as wide as saucers. "Uhhhhh. Okay." Blake threw the remains of his second PB&J into his pack and began struggling to pull it on.

"You get going. Head straight up the trail," Brice yelled. With one arm through one side of the pack and the other shoulder harness dangling, Blake took off up the path at a brisk pace.

By this time Brice had put the BLT back into the bear can and sealed the lid. He threw the bear can into his backpack. Then he remembered the bear pepper spray buried somewhere there. He thrust his hands deep into the pack, fumbling around to find the fire-extinguisher-shaped weapon. His fingers finally grasped what felt like the pepper-spray can. But something did not quite feel right. He yanked on the can to free it from the junk that had been packed in around it. Just as he got it out of the pack, he looked up to see the bear had already traveled about halfway across the meadow on a beeline right toward him. It was now only about fifty yards away.

Brice spun on his heels and grabbed his pack all in one motion. He threw it on his shoulders, yanked on the straps so it was tight to his body, and broke into a run as he headed up the trail after Blake.

At least I have the pepper spray, he thought. As he ran, he looked ahead and saw that the giant beast had veered toward the right and was now galloping parallel to Blake on the other side of the meadow. *Is he tracking Blake?*

I've got the get the pepper spray gun ready, he thought. He looked down at the spray can in his hand. He was dismayed.

Instantly he realized why the spray can had not felt quite right. When he packed the pepper-spray can into the backpack the night before, he had failed to take it out of the molded-plastic packaging. The packaging was perfect for retail stores to hang the can and display it. But now, as he tried to tear off the plastic, he realized this was going to be a big problem.

Tearing at the packaging with his bare hands got him nowhere. He began to bite at the packaging, trying to rip it open. All that got him was a mouthful of blood.

Great. I'm gonna get eaten alive because of some molded plastic packaging made in who-knows-where.

Knife. Where is a knife? he wondered, then remembered he had put a Swiss Army knife in the pouch that acted as the lid of the pack. In the same instant, he realized there was no time to fish for for it amid the dozen other items in that pouch. *But I've got to get that knife. If I don't have time to cut open the spray packaging, at least I could go for the bear's neck and give Blake a chance to get away.*

As Brice watched the bear tracking his thirteen-year-old son, he was screaming inside. He needed to get to Blake. He put his head down and broke into an all-out, adrenaline-fueled sprint.

There was no place to turn but up. This was one jam he needed help with.

He prayed out loud, "Lord, I ask you in the name of Jesus, protect us, help us out here. Lord, get rid of this bear!"

When he finally caught up to Blake, Brice looked back to where the bear had been. It was gone. The bear was *gone*.

After about another half mile of running at a good clip, they began to walk. A mile later, after making sure they were no longer being followed, the fear of the ordeal melted into laughter.

"You should have seen the look on your face, Dad," Blake said, shaking with laughing.

"*My* face? You should have seen *your* face. I thought your eyes were going to pop right out of your head."

Bear conquered. Check.

Everybody safe. Check.

Thank You, Lord.

GO TO THE MOUNTAIN

That trip was one Brice and Blake will never ever forget. Not only did it mark the change from boyhood to manhood for Blake, but the bond formed while they were on that mountain will never be broken. The days invested there were a rich time of adventure that left father and son admiring each other's qualities. From the day they returned, I saw a confidence in Blake that I had never seen before.

Watching that father-son trust relationship develop before my eyes taught me a lot about how our faith in our heavenly Father can spark and blossom when we deliberately leave our everyday lives behind and focus on Him. It's what I like to call going to the mountain. As I have studied the Scriptures to deepen my faith, I have become convinced that if we want to have ridiculous faith, we simply have to do this.

Great faith is always preceded by in-depth fellowship with our heavenly Father. The famous preacher Charles Spurgeon put it like this:

Would you, my brethren, have like faith, then walk in the same path [as Moses]. Be much in secret prayer. Hold constant fellowship with the Father, and with his Son Jesus Christ; so shall you soar aloft on wings of confidence, so shall you also open your mouth wide and have it filled with divine favors.[1]

What did Moses do? He went to the mountain. God invited Moses to come up to Mount Sinai, and he went.

When Moses went up on the mountain, the cloud covered it, and the glory of the LORD settled on Mount Sinai. For six days the cloud covered the mountain, and on the seventh day the LORD called to Moses from within the cloud. To the Israelites the glory of the LORD looked like a consuming fire on top of the mountain. Then Moses entered the cloud as he went on up the mountain. And he stayed on the mountain forty days and forty nights. (Ex. 24:15–18)

What was Moses doing on the mountain? The simple answer is he was connecting with God. He was having intense conversations and communion with God and deepening his relationship with his Creator. "The LORD would speak to Moses face to face as one speaks to a friend" (Ex. 33:11).

It is in such times of communion with God that we begin to see how trustworthy He is. And when we see His trustworthy character, our faith is transformed from fleeting to unwavering.

The reason Moses could have such great faith and be so strong in the face of overwhelming hardship was that he spent time on the mountain with God. There he saw God and "he persevered because he saw him who is invisible" (Heb. 11:27). After that experience on the mountain, Moses knew he could count on an invisible means of support. No matter what happened, whatever trials came his way, he could depend on this invisible God who had only become visible to him on the mountain.

When I say we need to go to the mountain, I reflect on one of my own adventures. I was supposed to go to Africa with Brice to meet our two sponsored African children (a story I detail in *Love, Skip, Jump*). But the night before we were supposed to leave, Brice got sick—I mean *really* sick. He couldn't go.

I was ready to cancel my trip, too, when he said, "Shelene, you're not sick. You need to go."

When I protested, he said, "God obviously wants to take a vacation with you."

I went. And that trip "to the mountain" changed my life. In Africa, for the first time, I was able to block out the noise of my life long enough to hear God's gentle whisper calling me to live differently. That trip compelled me to get my eyes off myself and start loving others as Christ did. It exploded my faith in ways I never could have imagined and led me to leave my life as a movie producer to found the charity Skip1.org, which funnels donations from ordinary people into food and water projects worldwide.[2]

I am convinced that those of us seeking to have great faith need to get seriously intentional about deepening our relationship with our Creator. That is impossible to do with this world constantly screaming at us. Amid the constant barrage of phone calls, e-mails, texts, likes, tweets, instant messages, Snapchats, friend requests, and automated reminders from the pharmacy to refill a prescription from two years ago we didn't know we had, it's no wonder we never have a chance to commune with God.

That's why we need mountain journeys in our lives. Times we can get away from it all, unplug, and be alone with God. It is only then, with all the demanding voices shut off, that we can turn to our Creator, who has become almost a stranger to us. It is only then that we can get reacquainted with the One who is letting us breathe. It is on the mountain that we can recognize how faithful He is. Only then can we grasp how worthy of our faith He is. Only then can He water the mustard seeds of faith that lie dormant deep within us.

When and where is your mountain? God beckons and invites you up. What are you going to do about His call?

Your mountain might be the beach, it might be a hotel room, it might be a campsite or simply a tent in your backyard. What matters is your decision to go there. To get away from your life long enough to connect with God.

You might say, "There is no way I can spare forty days." Okay, how about a week? How about starting with one single day? One day set aside to pray, worship, and reflect on God.

I have seen what God did when I climbed the mountain. I can promise you that your faith can't help but explode when you invest the time to seek and worship Him.

"Come near to God and he will come near to you" (James 4:8).

Lord, forgive me for letting the meaningless demands of this world drown out my pursuit of knowing and loving You. Forgive me for treating prayer as a task, an obligation

I must check off my list. Grant me the discipline to meet You on the mountain. When I am faced with trials that threaten to sink me, remind me that I have an invisible support that will sustain me. Build my faith so that I may please You with my life. Amen.

three

A VOICE FROM HEAVEN

By faith he left Egypt, not fearing the king's anger; he persevered because he saw him who is invisible.

—HEBREWS 11:27

Greg was only thirteen years old when he first learned his mother had breast cancer. It did not seem so terribly important to his young teenage mind. His mom said that she would be getting the latest treatments, that it was not something he should worry about. She was going to be just fine, and he believed her.

Not much changed at first. Greg went with her to a few doctor visits because the doctor's office was not far from his school. The changes in her were subtle at first. Then he began to notice how exhausted she looked, how she started to go to bed uncharacteristically early.

They did not discuss the radiation and chemotherapy

treatments, but Greg could see they were slowly wearing his mother down. One day a large clump of her hair fell out. He did not see her with hair again—not her hair anyway.

As the years went on, the treatments, postchemo sickness, and weariness almost became routine. Despite it all, Greg's mom made sure he was at every volleyball practice, every tournament. She attended every game possible despite the treatments and the side effects.

Then came the day when her tumors took her ability to walk and talk. She was in a strokelike state. The doctors said the breast cancer had metastasized. Her body was riddled with tumors, including a terrible one in her brain. Her bald head was marked with red ink to indicate where the radiation treatments were to be beamed—red ink that was permanently seared into his mind. As the disease began to win the battle, the doctors said there was nothing that could be done. Then, miraculously, she woke up for a few hours. She was actually able to carry on a conversation, just long enough to say good-bye to her seventeen-year-old son.

When the end came, the Lord was Greg's strength. His unanswered questions of why were soothed by the assurance that he would one day embrace his mother again. He knew in his soul that what others saw as the end was really only just a change. He was grateful for that and for the faith he'd seen her live out.

———

I first met Greg when he was twenty-three. He was a tall, handsome, athletic young man who had been a volleyball player in high school and college. He was kind, funny, a practical joker, and he wanted to date my twenty-year-old baby sister, Shanda. That meant he had to get my approval. But that wasn't hard, considering the way they met.

Greg's roommate, who was a mutual friend, kept hounding Shanda: "My roommate and you would be perfect together. You guys are *made* for each other! Let me set you up."

"Yeah, yeah, I hear this *all* the time. No thanks. I really don't want to date anyone right now," she would say.

"That's because you haven't met the right guy. I am telling you, you will change your mind when you meet him."

Shanda eventually relented, mostly just to pacify the matchmaking roommate. The blind date happened, and sparks instantly flew. Shanda and Greg were married within twelve months.

The matchmaker roommate happened to be a young Bible-college student named Francis Chan, who officiated his first wedding between his roommate, Greg, and my sister, Shanda.

———

It was May 2015. Greg was forty-three. He and Shanda were now parents of two beautiful girls—one fourteen, nearly the age he'd been when he found out about his mother's cancer, and the other one sixteen, close to the age he'd been when she died. The four of them lived only a few miles from where he'd grown up. And they were incredibly busy—especially Greg. This Saturday, in fact, was the first break he'd had in his schedule for months.

Spring was in full bloom. Mother's Day was a little more

than a week away and with the Southern California hills still green and full of wildflowers, Greg found himself thinking of his childhood—and his mom.

As he pulled his car onto the road at the end of his street, he could see the backside of the same mountains that stood at the end of his childhood backyard. Sweet memories of riding his bike on the mountain trails ran through his mind. He remembered playing in those mountains until it was almost dark and hurrying home before the last light disappeared. Mom would be coming up the path to find him.

Then he thought of the times he'd gotten in trouble in those mountains. Like the time he'd shot a horse's rear flank with his BB gun from three hundred yards away. That had seemed hilarious at the time. Who would have guessed the horse belonged to a police officer? His mother had grounded him for the summer, as any good mom would do. She'd explained to the officer that Greg was a good boy, just a little mischievous.

Then a disquieting thought disturbed his behind-the-wheel daydream. *Would I recognize her voice? Can I even remember what she sounded like?*

That night he confided in Shanda what he had been thinking. Shanda listened, gave him a hug, and said, "You don't need to remember your mom's voice to know she loves you and that someday you will see her again."

A few days later Greg received an unexpected voice mail from his cousin. "Hi, Greg, I have been going through and cleaning out some storage areas at my mom's, and I came across an old video of you and your mom. I uploaded it on Vimeo. I'll send you a link. I think you'll enjoy it."

That night Greg and Shanda sat down on their bed with his iPad. He opened the e-mail labeled July 25, 1984, and clicked the link. He tapped the "play" triangle on the video, not knowing what to expect. The screen blinked as the ancient video camera flickered on with a flash of fingerlike static. The video picture was tinted with the yellowish hue typical of 1980s camcorder technology.

Images of barely remembered faces—cousins, aunts, and uncles he had not seen in twenty-five years—began to flash across the screen. The camera slowly panned to an adolescent boy with braces. The boy smiled and waved at the camera. Greg smiled, remembering those painful braces. The boy on the screen was him. He was fifteen.

Suddenly the camera flickered off and then back on again, the slightly shaky picture indicating a less-experienced operator. His uncle's face appeared full frame. "Now you've got it on. Good job. Now see if you can zoom in on my face. . . . There you go. Now zoom back out." Greg realized that he was the cameraman getting instructions from his uncle.

The picture shifted floor to ceiling and then side-to-side while the camera was set up in a new position to capture the faces of family coming from the dining room. Then the image of an attractive woman in her early forties came into focus. She was walking right toward the camera and looking full frame into the lens. Her tender face peered out from the iPad screen at Greg as if she had been transported through time. There she was staring right at him.

"Are you running it?" she said in a sweet voice, noticeably uncomfortable when she realized she was being recorded. "Tell him not to run it," she said to her brother, who was out of the frame. Then the camera jerked to zoom in on her and she spoke Greg's name.

"Oh Greg—don't go so fast." It was the once-familiar voice that time had eroded from the corridors of his mind. But now that tender, sweet voice once again spoke his name—and it sent shivers down his spine. It was as if she were speaking to him right now.

He slid his finger on the screen to replay her words again: "Oh Greg—don't go so fast." A flood of tears began to stream down his cheeks. Shanda reached out and touched his arm in reassurance.

Had his mom known what his life had been like these past months? The hectic world he had been living in, with so little time for those things that really mattered. And now she was here with this message. Words spoken to keep a fifteen-year-old would-be cameraman from blurring the picture now struck him with a whole new meaning. It was a message from the lips of a loving mother, in a voice he barely recognized. A message about not letting life pass him by, about not letting the fast-tracked pace of this world dictate his actions. A much-needed message telling him to slow down, take time away, go to the mountain. A message that only the goodness of a good God could provide at the perfect time.

"Thank you, Lord," he whispered through happy tears. "Thank you for that good gift."

Sometimes we have drifted so far away from God we forget what His voice sounds like. Sometimes we have drifted so far we don't even recognize how far away we have gone. Instead of remembering God's quiet voice of wisdom, our ears are tantalized by meaningless messages of every kind. We can't help but have our attention consumed by the fire hose blasting us with an exhausting stream of endless messages from Twitter, Facebook, Instagram, and streaming everything. Don't get me wrong. The hundreds of selfies, videos, and tweets I sift through daily are quite entertaining. But too many times I have found myself making the excuse that I'm too busy to pray. Let's face it: our fast-paced, modern world is a faith-drowning disaster. We can't help but drift from the only anchor that will keep us safe.

But when we do go to the mountain, we have the privilege of experiencing God and remembering the sound of His voice. Through worship, prayer, and poring over His Word, we can connect to God. He can reveal His attributes. We can then begin to recognize His voice in our daily lives.

That's what happened to Moses when he went up the mountain. It had been three months since God had delivered the Israelites from Egypt. Three months since they had escaped by crossing the Red Sea. Moses had witnessed awesome demonstrations of God's goodness and the great faith of God's people—ridiculous faith that enabled them to walk on dry land through the Red Sea.

But even after those events, Moses needed to spend time alone with God. So here he was on the mountain. For forty amazing days he had listened to and bonded with his Creator. This was intimate friendship, and oh, how Moses needed that! He had been gone a long time, but he still did not want to leave.

Now, up to this point, God had chosen to show Himself to Moses in limited form—the only way a human could stand to encounter God "face to face" and "as one speaks to a friend" (Ex. 33:11). But Moses knew his God; he knew how powerful and majestic He is. He had experienced the amazing friendship of God, and now he wanted to know even more of God.

"Then Moses said, 'Now show me your glory'" (Ex. 33:18).

I have wondered how in the world Moses got the guts to ask God that. Had Moses lost his mind? Had he forgotten who he was dealing with? I imagine that the moment Moses uttered those words, he wished he hadn't. I am personally well accustomed to wishing I could take back words just leaving my lips. I suspect Moses felt the same way.

But to Moses' astonishment, God granted his request!

"And the LORD said, 'I will cause all my goodness to pass in front of you, and I will proclaim my name, the LORD, in your presence.' . . . 'But,' he said, 'you cannot see my face, for no one may see me and live'" (Ex. 33:19–20).

God in His wisdom granted Moses' request only partially. God agreed to show Moses one single aspect of His glory. Did God show Moses His holiness? His wisdom? His justice? His wrath? No. He chose to show Moses a tiny backside glimpse of His meekest, least terrifying attribute: His goodness.

"Then the LORD said, '. . . When my glory passes by, I will put you in a cleft in the rock and cover you with my hand until I have passed by. Then I will remove my hand and you will see my back; but my face must not be seen'" (Ex. 33:21–23).

The glory surrounding God's goodness was so intensely powerful that, to accommodate Moses' request, God took some serious protective measures so Moses wouldn't be vaporized.

He hid Moses in a cave and covered the opening of the cave with His hand to shield Moses from the complete impact of His goodness. Then he let Moses catch a tiny glimpse of His back as He was passing by.

I am convinced that what Moses saw was not just what his physical eyes could perceive. Human eyes cannot perceive things in the spiritual realm. In their fallen state, they're not meant to. What Moses saw was a split-second glimpse of the spiritual manifestation of a single characteristic of God. And even that tiny glimpse was most certainly the most epic vision any human has experienced in the history of humankind. Any filmmaker would give everything to have seen this masterpiece.

As the people of Israel stood at the foot of Mount Sinai, they looked up and witnessed lightning, thunder, fire, and earthquakes that rocked the mountain. Meanwhile, Moses was experiencing an amazing virtual-reality tour of God's goodness. I can imagine a rapid-fire THX surround-sound movie. Moses' senses were undoubtedly overwhelmed, even with God shielding him. Millions of images of the goodness of God passed before Moses. God's goodness in speaking creation into existence with an explosive thundering bang. His goodness in providing a perfectly mixed breath of air for each and every creature on this earth. The spectacular goodness of beauty in creation: verdant meadows, majestic mountains, crystal-clear lakes, and flowing rivers and waterfalls.

All this goodness passed in lightning succession before Moses' eyes. Yet God's revelation was not finished. It had hardly begun because His goodness transcends physical creation and reaches down into every individual life. Because God is not bound by time, Moses got to see millennium after millennium of goodness. The cross, God's provision for forgiveness of sins. God's amazing patience and grace. His thousands of daily little gifts of goodness in billions of human lives. That kind word, that warm hug, that link to a long-forgotten video of a beautiful tender face, that precious recording of a mother's voice, which time had eroded from a loving son's mind.

God's goodness passed before Moses, and Moses was forever changed. God's goodness passed before Greg Weaver, and he broke down and wept.

———

If you and I saw God in person, faith would no longer be our problem. If we actually saw God, we would be so blown away by the immensity of His presence and the unimaginable enormity of His existence, every doubt we have ever had would instantaneously melt away forever. Just like Moses, we would be left prostrate in awe of Jehovah. If we merely glimpsed Him passing by, we would drop everything and be ready and willing to do anything He asked. Our lives would radically change.

MEETING WITH GOD CHANGES YOU

"When Moses came down from Mount Sinai . . . he was not aware that his face was radiant because he had spoken with the LORD . . . and they were afraid to come near him" (Ex. 34:29–30).

Moses actually had to wear a veil over his head to keep from freaking people out. That's what happens when we start spending time with God on the mountain. We are changed, and people see it.

If we desire to have ridiculous faith, we have to do some serious talking with and listening to God. That fellowship with God is like fuel for our souls. It will embolden our prayer lives, it will empower our beliefs, and it will minister to our spirits. We need it. We can't operate properly without it, and our faith will never become empowered if we don't personally experience our absurdly, unbelievably good God.

> Lord, Your goodness is more than I can comprehend. I am humbled that You have been so good to me—I don't deserve this goodness. Don't allow me to drift so far that I fail to recognize Your voice. Build in my heart a burning desire to meet with You on the mountain. Meet me there so that I may deepen my understanding of Your awesome goodness and my knowledge of Your amazing nature. Amen.

part two

SEEKING THE FACE OF JESUS

I have learned that to have ridiculous faith we need to seek the face of Jesus. I remember a time when I would say, "Oh, I already do that. I go to church, Bible study, and small group. Of course I seek the face of Jesus." But that's not what I am talking about. I love the church, and I am not devaluing those things. But I am afraid that, just like the religious leaders of Jesus' time, we can do all the religious things and still miss Him.

You see, Jesus has always appeared in the most unexpected ways. He was seen in the most unexpected places. When the King of the universe came from His heavenly home to this earth, He came as an unassuming peasant child. He could have come with all the power of heaven in a mighty thunderstorm

or arrived at the gates of Jerusalem with a cohort of angel warriors. He could have come like that, but He did not.

So where will we find Jesus? Look in the faces of those who need help. The hungry. The thirsty. Those needing clothes. Those who are sick or are in prison. Jesus said, "Whatever you did for one of the least of these brothers and sisters of mine, you did for me" (Matt. 25:40).

When I got out of my comfortable church seat to see Jesus where He said He would be, my faith begin to change, radically change. Because for the first time in my life I began to find Him.

four

A FULL CAR

*If I have a faith that can move mountains, but
do not have love, I am nothing. If I give all
I possess to the poor and give over my body
to hardship that I may boast, but do not have
love, I gain nothing.*

—1 CORINTHIANS 13:2–3

Several years ago I was faced with my own excess and greed
during the Christmas season and determined that, from then on,
Christmas was going to be about others, not gluttonous materialism. I had also been learning about how God has called us to
live out a life of love. As a result, for the past several years our
family has volunteered as guest chefs for Christmas breakfast at
a homeless shelter in Glendale, California. A few years ago, as
the holiday season approached, our son, Blake, asked if he could
invite his teammates from the varsity basketball team at Oaks
Christian School to decorate the shelter for Christmas.

"Mom," Blake explained, "that way we can get to know

the children and families who will be there Christmas morning when we cook breakfast."

I loved the idea and told Blake to set it up with the coach and players. On November 22, six very large basketball players piled into my SUV, and we carpooled down to the shelter with several other cars loaded with everything you could imagine: a Christmas tree, lights, stockings, gingerbread houses, candy canes, and even a plastic snowman.

I gave each basketball player a Target gift card and told them to pick one child or parent during our time at the shelter and to bless them with this gift card.

We walked in with our arms filled with decorations and our hearts full of joy. Some of the players were a bit unsure at first, but as they got busy putting up the tree and decorations, the children at the shelter started warming up to them. Soon the players were working right along with the children from the shelter, decorating and having a blast.

I looked across the room and absorbed a scene that made me smile. Several young men were building gingerbread houses with little girls. Others were helping young boys string lights on the tree. At the same time, shelter moms were personalizing Christmas stockings for their children.

When the decorating was done, Blake had the idea to play their own version of the singing talent show *The Voice*. Soon four basketball players were sitting in swiveling office chairs as judges. The children and teens in the shelter then took turns singing their lungs out. It wasn't long before a crowd gathered to hear surprisingly good entertainers. The Oaks Christian guys would swivel their chairs around and start fighting over the "contestants."

"I want you on my team!"

Another judge would spin around and say, "No! I want you on my team."

A verbal battle then ensued, something along the lines of "You don't want him. He'll ruin your career!"

"Oh, yeah? Well, I dare you to ask *him* to sing and then tell me if you want him to be your mentor!"

The children sang, the parents laughed, and for a moment you couldn't tell who was from the shelter and who was from Oaks Christian School.

As I was cracking up at a six-foot-five-inch muscular basketball player attempting to play the part of Christine Aguilera, I noticed a volunteer I did not recognize working with several of the young kids to make the Christmas crafts we had brought. Assuming she was a fellow volunteer, I went over to introduce myself.

"Hi, I'm Shelene," I said with a smile.

"I'm Wanda. Thanks for coming with these boys."

Suddenly I realized this woman was not a volunteer at all and the group of children surrounding her were not random children from the shelter. They were *her* kids.

We were soon engaged in conversation, and I learned that Wanda Rendell was living at the shelter with her husband and their seven kids.

At first she was guarded—very careful with her words. But I sat with her mom to mom, and soon she relaxed. We talked about what all moms talk about—our kids. I introduced her to Blake. She introduced me to her husband, Terrence, and to their seven children—Terrence Jr. (fifteen), Whitney (fourteen), Willow (thirteen), TJ (eight), Wendi (seven), Wynne (five), and Theo (three)—and briefly shared her story.

Six months earlier they had lost their house and had started living in their minivan. With seven kids, they'd had to take turns sleeping inside the crammed car. Blankets on the seats and pillows piled on the floorboards became their beds. Her husband and their oldest son, Terrence Jr., would sleep outside on cots to guard the family. In the mornings a trip to the local McDonalds gave the kids a chance to straighten disheveled clothes and to brush their teeth before school. The kids' classmates never knew.

As we talked, my heart was breaking for this mom. What a devastating experience. And yet Wanda seemed remarkably upbeat and hopeful.

As the night was winding down, I told my new friend that we would be back Christmas morning and that I looked forward to seeing her and her husband and having them meet the rest of my family.

"That's really nice," she said, "but I don't plan on still being here by Christmas. The shelter is trying to help us get housing."

"Well, either way. Whether you are still here or in your new home, I'd really like the rest of my family to meet you and your husband and kids. Here's my e-mail and cell number."

"Okay, I will contact you."

"Oh, and Wanda, please let me know when you find housing."

That night on our way home, the basketball guys were talking nonstop about who they had given their gift cards to and how they had fallen in love with the children at the shelter. Most of the young men had never been to a homeless shelter before. They were rocked, really rocked.

As Thanksgiving quickly approached, I couldn't get the Rendell family off my heart or out of my thoughts.

On December 4, 2013, I received the following e-mail from my new friend Wanda.

Hello Shelene,

I am Wanda. My family met you at Ascencia. I just wanted to send you a thank-you e-mail for the spirit your organization brought to Ascencia. I really appreciate how your team embraced my children. As a wife and a mother it's been a long time since I've been able to see my husband relax and laugh if just for a moment with the coach and the guys from the basketball team. My daughter still talks about "The Voice" and your son. But, your basketball team had the biggest impact on my oldest son. Here, he doesn't have anyone to relate to. Just to see him laughing, joking and being a teenager again was priceless to me. That was the best Christmas present ever. Everyone was just a joy to be around. (Young men spending their Friday night decorating a shelter just touched my heart.) Terrence Jr. asks all the time did I get the guys' basketball schedule. I know you're extremely busy but I would love to take him to a home basketball game because he's never had that experience before. I'm not going to take up any more of your time. I just wanted to say THANK-YOU SOOOOOOO MUCH.

From,

The Rendell Family

As I finished reading the e-mail, tears were streaming down my face. My heart was so full of love for this mother and her sweet family.

That night I could not sleep. I kept thinking of the Rendells in the shelter, with mom and dad hardly sleeping, watching guard over their kids. The next morning, I hit the forward button on my e-mail and sent Wanda's e-mail to the Oaks Christian varsity basketball coach and the team mom, Michelle.

Michelle e-mailed me back almost instantly.

Okay, I'm in love with this woman. Could we appoint her son to be honorary team manager for a game? We could introduce him in the starting lineup and let him run through the boys with a high five at the end!

This is too priceless and important to set aside as a nice thank-you note. Mark and I will sponsor a limo to pick Terrence Jr. and the family up and bring them to a game if the coach thinks we can do something special here.

Within two days Michelle's idea to have Terrence Jr. act as an honorary basketball manager for our first home game got approved by everyone. I then was given the awesome opportunity of e-mailing Wanda the news and inviting her family to the game.

Hi, Wanda . . . Your e-mail brought tears to my eyes. Thank you for sharing your family with us. The guys on the basketball team have not stopped talking about your family. We would like to do something special for your son Terrence Jr. Our first league home game is on Jan. 5. We'd like to send a driver to pick up your entire family and bring you all to the game and then have dinner after with the team. I feel so blessed to have met you, my new friend. As I told you last month, our family and friends will be at Ascencia on Christmas morning as the guest chefs. I can't wait for you to meet my husband, Brice, and daughter, Brooke. Please call or e-mail me anytime if you need anything.

Merry Christmas & God Bless, Shelene

The next day I received Wanda's e-mail response:

OH MY GOSH!!! Thank you soooooooooo much. Terrence Jr.'s birthday is Jan. 5. This is going to be the most awesome birthday gift EVER. Then I will be crowned the coolest mom in the entire world. Thank you. Thank you. Thank you. Sooooooo much.

Did you get that? Terrence Jr.'s birthday was January 5. Of course it was. I love how God rolls. When I called Wanda at the shelter, I could feel us hugging each other through the phone. It was awesome. "Shelene, please do not tell anyone about this," she said. "I am going to keep this a secret and a special surprise for Terrence Jr., seeing how there aren't that many exciting things happening in his life right now."

I promised to keep quiet.

As Christmas Day approached, I was a little worried that the Rendells might not find a place to live by Christmas as they hoped. The first night I met Wanda, she'd told me they had found a home to rent. But later she said they had been to see the place, and it was disgusting. Trash was piled everywhere, exposed electrical cords powered the lighting, the carpet was stained, and the whole place smelled like dead rats.

The slumlord had promised the Rendells that the house would be completely gutted and that new carpet and paint would be finished by the Friday before Christmas. But as Friday grew closer, Wanda confided that she and Terrence were not telling the kids about the house. They had been let down too many times by landlords who made promises and did not follow through.

Wise woman, I thought.

Before she left for her appointment at the house, Wanda called me. "If the landlord does everything he said—clean out the piles of trash, paint, and replace the carpet, we will be getting the keys today," she said with a hint of excitement.

"If he's letting you go there, I'm sure it's fine. If it's not ready, I'm sure he would have called and canceled," I reassured her.

"Yes, you're right."

Saturday morning I called Wanda.

"Well, did you get it? Are you guys moving in?"

There was momentary silence on the other end of the line.

"No, Shelene. The trash was still piled on the carpet, and nothing had been done." I could hear the tired disappointment in her voice.

"The worst part is that the voucher for our housing assistance approval is supposed to run out at the end of the month, and with Christmas everything is shutting down."

With Christmas just a week away, her family still being in the shelter for the holiday was a sad, gripping reality. Yet her strength was humbling. Every time I'd call her, she was brave, and not a tear was shed. She asked for nothing. She knew the verse in the Bible that said a wise woman builds her house and a foolish one tears it down with her own hands. She also knew seven sets of eyes, ages three to fifteen, were watching her. She had no choice but to have faith. Faith the size of a mustard seed, perhaps. Ridiculous faith! But she believed that kind of faith could move mountains.

A few days before Christmas, Jasmine Hainer, a young girl I had been mentoring, contacted me. She had heard about the basketball team decorating the homeless shelter in November. She wanted to serve. She asked if her family could join us Christmas morning.

I said, "Yes, of course. You are welcome to join us, but be sure to ask your family first."

A lot of families I know already have their Christmas morning traditions, and being guest chefs at a homeless shelter is not one of the top ten traditions.

When Christmas morning arrived, Blake was the first one awake at our house. He was extremely excited to get to the shelter and see his new friend Terrence Jr.

When we arrived at the shelter, Jasmine, her sister, brother, and mom and dad were waiting outside. Love does that. As a family, they were stepping out to maybe find a new holiday tradition.

The moment we entered the shelter, everyone jumped into their jobs as if they had been serving side by side with us for years. Someone started the coffee. Another friend, who is an amazing chef, started cooking the eggs and bacon. A few more started on the waffles. But I was focused on finding one person: Wanda Rendell.

I had been thinking of her from the moment I woke up that Christmas morning. I had been thinking how Brice and I used to fill the kids' stockings or stay up late to build the Barbie dream house or put together the basketball hoop. We would set out the cookies and milk for Santa and sprinkle "reindeer food" on the grass for Rudolph. With those thoughts flying through my head, the Rendells' situation hit me hard. The reality was that they were not filling stockings or putting together gifts to be placed under their tree or setting out cookies for Santa.

As I searched the ground floor for Wanda, I prayed silently: *Lord, forgive me. Forgive me for even thinking those things matter. Please perform a Christmas miracle for the Rendells today. Let Brice's heart feel the same peace I feel about this family. Use us, Lord, as You see fit.*

It wasn't long before the smells of Christmas breakfast filled the air, and the guests living at the shelter began making their way to the dining area. When Wanda came down, I locked eyes with her immediately, and a huge smile spread across my face.

"Woohoo!" I squealed as I raised my hands in excitement and ran over to Wanda. We gave each other big hugs. I immediately introduced her to Brice and Brooke. By then her husband and some of their younger kids had joined us, and we all grabbed a table to sit and have Christmas breakfast together. Brice and Terrence talked for hours as the kids laughed and played, and he learned a little more about their situation.

Brice found out that Terrence had been in the real estate business, flipping homes, before losing everything in the economic disaster of 2008. They'd ended up living in the car because they had no family in town and no friends in a position to help a family of nine. It had been a blessing to get off the streets and into this shelter, where they had a roof over their heads and could count on three meals day.

The shelter also has resources like computers and Internet

access to assist in finding homes and jobs. But it's a temporary solution. Guests are allowed to stay three months and are then required to leave. The Rendells' time was up and there was an unspoken pressure for the family to get out. Every potential rental they had found had been a disaster or was not approved by the assistance program.

As the breakfast was winding down, we had one last surprise for the family.

During a phone conversation, I had asked Wanda a question. "If you could have one wish (besides a home) on Christmas Day, what would it be?"

Her reply had been instant. "Sleep. Sleep. Since being in the shelter," she'd explained, "especially with seven kids, you never close your eyes completely. Terrence and I sleep with one eye open all night. So many people come in and out of this place, and I don't trust anyone."

As we sat with the family now, I handed Terrence an envelope. "We have booked adjoining rooms for your family at Embassy Suites. There's a free breakfast in the morning and a pool for the kids. It's time that you guys get some real rest."

"*What?*" Wanda said. "Are you serious?"

"Yes, I'm serious, and our group here this morning will also be giving you a prepaid credit card for you and your family to have Christmas dinner together tonight wherever you'd like to go."

With that our good-byes were said, wishes for a Merry Christmas were given. But our faith ride with the Rendells had just begun.

On the drive home Brice shared that, after meeting Terrence and Wanda and their kids, he felt we absolutely needed to do whatever we could to help them get out of the homeless shelter. That Christmas night as we gathered with the rest of our extended family and friends for dinner, the Rendells were the talk of the night.

God was teaching me that a life of faith involves living out love. True love is not empty "do good" actions motivated by how generous we will look to others so that we can boast with pride. I am convinced the life of faith and love God wants from us is a life that loves others the way He loves us.

And that sometimes requires ridiculous faith.

Lord, give me the strength to love as You love. I do not want to do anything with selfish ambition or vain conceit. Help me to live a life that notices those who are in need of a helping hand to get back on their feet. Help me to welcome them, care for them, and love them. Amen.

five

A FULL HOUSE

*And now these three remain: faith, hope and
love. But the greatest of these is love.*
—1 Corinthians 13:13

The Christmas season flew by. The New Year rang in with
a bang. January 5 came before anybody expected. That was
the night Terrence Jr. would be Oaks Christian School's honorary varsity basketball manager for the first home game.

School spirit was flying high at home that night.

The gym was packed with fans excited to cheer on the new
season. The team had several returning starters, and a fer-
vent buzz of anticipation filled the air. Lecrae's powerful lyrics
blasted through the subwoofer speakers, and everybody was
having fun waiting for things to get started. Then the music
faded, the cheerleaders made a tunnel down the middle of the
gym floor, and the announcer started his spiel. "Ladies and
gentlemen, *welcome* to the Oaks Christian varsity basketball
season. Tonight we have a starting lineup for you . . ."

The starters ran through the group of screaming cheerleaders as each of their names was called. They gave high fives and performed timed jumps with their teammates. The last name announced was Terrence Jr.'s. He ran through the lineup tunnel and exchanged a *huge* chest bump with one of the players at the end of the tunnel.

Terrence Jr. performed his manager duties during the first half like a champ. During halftime the dance and cheer teams performed a rousing number and then sang a surprise happy birthday song just for Terrence Jr. His smile shined all the way across the gym—I think it had a little more to do with the cheerleader singers than the song itself!

The team had an amazing night on the floor, and the strong victory put everybody in a great mood. After the game, Vince Daily, one of the OC School dads, came up to Brice and asked about the family we sat with at the game and the young boy sitting on the bench as the honorary basketball manager. Brice shared their story, and Vince said, "Call Monday. I might have a job for the dad, it's not a sure thing, but I have a new construction project my company is possibly going to be starting and there is a good chance I will need him in a few weeks."

"Okay. Sounds good," Brice said.

In the car Brice told me about his conversation with Vince about a possible job for Terrence.

"They live in Glendale and go to school in downtown LA, honey. Terrence can't take a job out here; it's thirty miles away." I said.

"Well," Brice said, "why can't they move out here? Remember I told you about my client who has a four-bedroom, three-bath house for rent?"

"That's still available?" I asked.

"I don't know," Brice answered, "but I'm going to find out."

"Their housing assistance is only good in the City of Glendale. The City of Glendale is not going to let that money leave their city and come to ours. I know—"

I stopped midsentence. Brice was smiling at me. Raising objections was not usually my role. He was usually the one trying to curtail one of *my* harebrained ideas. The look on his face showed he was obviously enjoying the role reversal.

"Brice, don't look at me like that. I get it. I know I sound negative, but I'm not negative. I'd love for the Rendells to get that house. That would be amazing. But they have had their hearts broken so many times, and I don't want them to get their hopes up for nothing."

"Honey," Brice said, "don't worry. You're married to a lawyer, remember. Let me handle the City of Glendale. The fact is, Glendale just doesn't have housing available for a family of nine. They've been looking for four months with no success whatsoever. I just need to work that angle. Meanwhile, why don't you see if Skip1 can help with getting donations for beds, furniture, and appliances."

"Is your client even open to renting his place to the Rendells?"

"I don't know, but I am meeting with him Monday, so we shall see," Brice said.

"Wow—you've been busy, Brice."

"That's what love does," he said.

Do you see why I married this man?

When Brice got home Monday evening, I pounced without taking a breath.

"What did your client say about the house? Did you hear

from the city? What did Vince say about the job? When do you think we can show the Rendells the house?"

"Shelene, slow down, honey. One question at a time."

As you can tell, I get a little excited.

"Well, honey," Brice said, "my client said—" He paused for dramatic effect. "*Yes*, he is open to taking a section 8 voucher for the rent."

"*What?* Awesome!" I squealed.

"That's not all," Brice said. "He will even reduce the rent a bit so we can make it work. I have several calls in to the City of Glendale, and they are working right now to see if they can get it approved. Oh, and I called Terrence. He and Wanda are going to look at the house tonight."

"*Wow!* That's amazing. Did they freak out?"

"Pretty much," Brice said. "But they are not telling their kids because the city is still the unknown factor. We won't know if it's going to work until we hear from them. And I have to tell you, it's looking like a long shot right now. Glendale has never done anything like this before."

As Brice finished his sentence, fourteen-year-old Brooke walked into the kitchen. She had overheard the conversation and said, "God is going to give the Rendells this house, Mommy."

"Really? Brookie, that's sweet. We sure hope so."

"No, Mom, I'm serious. I prayed and asked God to give them this house, and I have faith that He will do it."

"Brooke, that's great, sweetheart, but God is not a genie or fairy godmother."

"I know, Mom. But the Bible says if we have faith, even faith as small as a mustard seed, we can move mountains."

"But Brooke, it might not be His will for the Rendells to be in this house."

"Have faith, Mom. I feel a peace about it. God will do what He wants, and I believe He wants them out of that shelter."

As Brooke finished her inspirational mini-sermon, Brice's cell phone rang. He stepped outside to take the call. As he walked back in, Brooke asked, "Was that the city?"

"Yes, yes, it was. How did you know that? Anyway, great news. This is unprecedented—they have never done this before. They are going to extend the voucher. If the Rendells want the home, it just needs to pass inspection, and they can move in."

"*What?*" I said. "This is so awesome."

Brooke looked me right in the eyes and said, "Like you say, Mom. God is in the *victory* business."

"Yes, He is, honey. Yes, He is."

As I'm sure you can imagine, the Rendells loved, loved, loved the house. It was a four-bedroom, three-bath, two-story at the end of a quiet cul-de-sac, and it was in a blue-ribbon school district. The city inspector came out and was thrilled with the property. It passed with flying colors.

Terrence had a talk with Brice and expressed his big concern—his employment status. "The last thing I want to do is get into this house only to lose it because I don't have a job."

"Well, Terrence, we are going to pray about that and trust that God is going to do something."

That night Brice and I spent time praying over the Rendells' situation. "Lord, we give this whole situation to You. You have burdened our heart for this family, and we pray You will make this all work out for them. We know You have the power to do this, and we just ask, if this be Your will, that You make the impossible happen."

The next day Brice got a call from Vince Daily. Their conversation in the gym had been about two weeks earlier.

"Brice, Vince here. Remember that homeless family's dad? What was his name?"

"Terrence."

"Yes, Terrence, that's it. Is he still looking for work?"

"Yes," Brice said, "actually he is. And God willing, if he gets a job, they are going to move into a home just five miles from us."

"That's amazing! Have him call me. My company just picked up that new project I was telling you about and I think I have something for him."

"Are you kidding me?" Brice said, remembering the prayers from the night before. "I will do that."

Terrence called and was hired the next day. Terrence works seven days a week from 5:00 p.m. to 5:00 a.m. doing security for Vince's construction company. Not a lazy bone in this man's body!

———

As the reality of a home hit Terrence and Wanda, they were overwhelmed. It seemed too good to be true. A home. And not just any home. This one had room for all nine of them. Did they really have a place of their own, a place for their family?

It was not long before my cell phone began to ring constantly as word spread around the school that the Rendells had a home.

The first call was from Anders Heiner. Anders was the dad of the girl I had been mentoring, the family who had gone with us Christmas morning. Anders and his wife, Julie, had been rocked by their experience at the shelter. They were calling to check on the Rendells. I excitedly shared the latest news.

"What are they going to do for furniture?" Anders asked.

"I know they have a small storage unit, but they don't have any beds."

"Well, Shelene, we would like to buy them all beds."

I gulped, thinking of the cost. "Beds for all nine of them?"

"Yes. Well, how about eight? We can let Terrence and Wanda sleep together!"

"That sounds wonderful. They will be thrilled!"

When I said "beds," I was thinking mattresses. But Anders was thinking the works: bed frames, mattresses, mattress covers, sheets, bedspreads, bed skirts, pillows, bath towels, washcloths, and so forth.

I hung up, in awe of what God was doing. Then my dear friend Michelle called.

"Shelene, I heard about the house for the Rendells. That is amazing. What do they need?"

"Hmmm, they have no fridge and no way to wash their clothes," I said.

"Well," she said, "Mark and I would like to get the Rendells a washing machine and a dryer and a refrigerator."

"Oh, my gosh, this is so awesome. Thank you, Michelle. They are going to freak out!"

———

The next day was move-in day, and we could not wait to help. The older kids had never seen the house, and the disbelief on their faces was a beautiful sight.

We began assembling the new bunk beds, the lamps, and other items. Once the beds were assembled, we were all congregating in the upstairs central hallway, in happy discussion about the sheets, pillows, bedspreads, and other new household items, when chimes rang throughout the house. Everyone froze and looked at one another.

"Isn't somebody going to answer the door?" I asked as the doorbell rang again.

Willow immediately bolted downstairs to the door, then she stopped and looked up at her dad. "Can I answer it?"

"Yes, of course, answer it!" he said, nodding with a smile on his face.

As the door opened, Blake, who had come from a basketball game, entered the house. "Aaaayyyy!"

Hugs abounded. Then three-year-old Theo ran up to Blake: "Blaaaake, I got a bed!" he shouted with pure joy. He thrust his little hand into Blake's much bigger one and led him up the stairs to proudly show Blake his new sleeping quarters.

Later that night, when all the finishing touches were complete, I walked by fourteen-year-old Whitney's open door. She was looking at herself in the mirrored closet door and quietly singing in rhythmic time, "I have a be-ed, I have a be-ed, I have my own bed."

The Rendells were finally at home.

We brought over two of our folding tables and nine folding chairs so the family could have a table to eat on. There was very little other furniture, but nobody cared.

The next morning, Wanda started working on enrolling the kids into their new schools.

———

On February 26, I got a text from one of Brooke's friends:

Hey, it's Olivia. My whole family has been sorting and we have 5 boxes of clothes and a couple of pieces of furniture. We wanted to see if you have a charity or something we could donate them to. If not, we were thinking of a garage sale. Last time we raised $3,800. We could donate to Skip1.org.

I texted back:

WOW!! That's huge and amazing! What type of furniture do you have? Skip1 just recently put a homeless family that we met over Christmas in a home. They need a couch and table. They have been using our folding table to eat at. Other than beds they have no other furniture. Thank you for thinking of Skip1. You guys are amazing.

Olivia texted back:

My mom said she'll get back to you later on with what she has.

I texted:

Perfect.

About an hour later, Olivia's mom, Margret, called me. I told her about the Rendells needing furniture. She asked me if they were the family from the basketball game.

"Yes," I said, remembering that was the night two of her daughters were cheerleading for the game. They had sung "Happy Birthday" to Terrence Jr.

"Would you like to meet Wanda and see where they're living?" I asked.

"Yes, I'd love to," Margret said.

I called Wanda. She said to come on over. Soon we were knocking on the Rendells' door. Wanda invited us in, and we stepped into her large, completely empty living room—not a single piece of furniture. Margret looked thoughtful as Wanda showed us around the sparsely furnished home.

After we left, Margret and I went to lunch. She kept that thoughtful look while she ate. Then she told me that this Sunday she wanted to send the Rendell family out to lunch and then to a movie. "Once they are gone, I will back up a moving truck and completely furnish their downstairs."

"But Olivia said you might just have a couple of pieces of furniture!"

"No," Margret said. "That will not do. Now that I see the space and their needs . . . just meet me at the house on Sunday."

I agreed.

When Sunday rolled around, Margret, her three girls, and a couple of their friends came to join Blake and me at the Rendells' home.

The Rendells were away enjoying breadsticks and Italian food and after they ate were going to see a movie.

Right on time, the moving truck backed into the driveway. We began moving in a truckload of beautiful items that could have come right out of a Pottery Barn catalog.

A beautiful love seat tucked under the bay window. Then came a gorgeous leather chair with ottoman, coffee tables, lamps, and artwork. A dining-room table that seated twelve. Dishes, silverware, candles, glasses, tablecloths, and more completed the delivery.

I have seen things like this happen on reality shows like *Room Raiders* or *Divine Design*, but never up close and personal. It all happened within a three-and-a-half-hour window.

When Wanda Rendell and her children opened the front door to their home, she went weak at the knees. She was speechless. How could a woman she had met just a few days earlier be extending this kind of kindness? It was ridiculous.

It is important to mention here that the help provided to the Rendells was not about materialism. It was not about the quality of the furniture or the size of the accommodations. Indeed, the Rendell family would have been happy with any roof over their heads and just a floor to sleep on. This was about a family of faith in need and a community freely opening their hands to love and provide.

Because of the willingness of some high school boys to give up their Friday night to lend a hand at a homeless shelter, nine people were rescued. Nine family members who had experienced persecution, been ridiculed for their faith, and endured more than their fair share of hardship.

Through it all God had been teaching all of us about living a life of faith and showing His love. Through the amazing privilege of loving and doing life with the Rendell family, God spoke to my heart: *Shelene, do you see how this works? Your life of love is My answer to somebody else's prayer of faith.*

I have learned that to have ridiculous faith we need to seek the face of Jesus. You see, Jesus has always appeared in the most unexpected ways. He came quietly, meekly, with only a few shepherds and barnyard animals to celebrate the King's entrance into our world. And He shows up today in the most unexpected places.

So where do we find the face of Jesus? We will find Him where He said we would find Him. "They also will answer, 'Lord, when did we see you hungry or thirsty or a stranger or needing clothes or sick or in prison, and did not help you?' He will reply, 'Truly I tell you, whatever you did not do for one of the least of these, you did not do for me'" (Matt. 25:44–45).

———

When I think of what God did with the Rendell family, I can't help but picture three-year-old Theo sitting with his little legs stretched out in his red Radio Flyer wagon, with a giant smile on his face, in the driveway of the home that God had provided on a mustard seed of faith.

Little had I known, when I got out of my comfortable church seat to seek the face of Jesus, that my faith would begin to explode.

Little had I understood that faith really can move a mountain, even when that mountain takes the form of a family trusting God and a little boy sitting in a red wagon.

Dear God, I see how faith and love work together. Thank You for letting me be a tiny part of what You want to do for Your children. Thank You for letting me witness firsthand Your steadfast faithfulness and Your beautiful guiding hand of providence and for letting me see You in the face of a little boy with a big smile. Amen.

six

COOLIO'S FAITH WALK

*Now faith is confidence in what we hope for
and assurance about what we do not see.*
—HEBREWS 11:1–2

The last two days of my ten-day trip to Uganda featured a safari in Queen Elizabeth National Park. The purpose was to decompress after an intense week of visiting villages and feeding children. If you ever have the opportunity to fly all the way to Africa, be sure you make time for at least one safari. I'm sure you won't regret it.

I almost regretted it, though, when the puddle-jumper plane began to drop out of the sky toward a grass field. In fact, I pretty much freaked out.

"What's he doing?" I cried to the passenger in the seat next to mine. The plane was getting dangerously close to the ground. "There's no runway down there!"

Our guide from the orphanage flashed a huge, pearly

white smile."No problem, Momma Shelene. He lands us on the grass."

Needless to say, my knuckles were white from clawing onto the metal seat as the oversized airplane tires bumped down onto the grassy field.

"See, Momma Shelene, I told you. No problem."

"No problem for you," I said with a relieved chuckle, "but I just about had a heart attack!"

As I exited the plane onto our "runway," I could see the Mweya Airport was just a flat, grassy, wide-open field on the beautiful African savanna. The resort employees had lined up to greet us as if we were on an episode of *Fantasy Island* (young people—look it up). Friendly smiles and welcomes abounded.

We were escorted into the lobby of the resort to await our room assignments. It was not long until my roommate, Mary, and I had a key and a room number and a bellman to do the heavy lifting. I liked this place already!

That feeling left as quickly as it had come when we were walking down the outdoor path to our room and a huge giraffe walked right across our path. Now, I had seen many giraffes before—*in a zoo*. They were all about half the size of this guy. Most important, they were always behind a carefully planned and meticulously built and maintained barrier fence. Startled, I looked anxiously at the bellman as if to say "save me," but he just looked back with a calm smile.

"Let me guess," I said, "no problem, right?"

He smiled and shrugged. "They lived here first," he said as if he did not have a care in the world.

As we proceeded farther along the path to our room, I heard a sound like someone snoring. I looked over at Mary for a touch of reassurance, only to see her eyes go wide with fear. She was staring at something behind me. I spun around, only to come face-to-face with an enormous warthog. It had to be the source of the giant snort we had heard seconds earlier. This was not a cute, smiling, animated Pumba-type warthog ready to do a tap dance and serenade us with a rousing rendition of "Hakuna Matata." This guy had six-inch white tusks angrily protruding from the sides of his mouth, and he looked ready to gore us just for the fun of it.

"Aaahh!" I blurted out in sheer surprise. At this, the warthog appeared to size us up with a stare and grunted off into the bushes. That was heart attack number two within twenty minutes.

We had better get to our room and lock the door, I thought. Then, out loud, I said to Mary, "And this was supposed to be relaxing!"

Our luggage was loaded into our room, and the bellman said, "Your group is scheduled for a 'chimp hike' first thing tomorrow morning. Please meet in the lobby at eight o'clock."

"Okay. Great. Thank you," I said as I quickly shut and double-bolted the door.

The next morning came quickly. I slept so soundly that when the front desk called our room, I jumped.

We met our group in the lobby at eight sharp.

Nine of us piled into two Land Rovers and headed out to the start of our "chimp hike." The driver dropped us off at the edge of a cliff overlooking a giant valley rain forest. One of the guides explained that this was Kyambura Gorge on the eastern side of the park.

As I looked over the edge of the valley, I thought, *Wow,*

that's really far down. I would never have dreamed in a million years that where I was looking was where we would be taking our hike.

Our group was split into two and my group was assigned a guide named Coolio. Coolio was about five-foot-nine and weighed maybe 130 pounds dripping wet. He was decked out in army-green military fatigues, complete with a Ugandan flag patch sewn onto the left sleeve. Slung by a strap over his left shoulder was a not-so-clean AK-47 rifle.

Will that thing even fire? I wondered, imagining the beasts we might encounter as we descended the jungle-lined red-dirt path.

Coolio's outfit was topped off by a matching militia cap with a white patch on the front, indicating he was an official guide for Queen Elizabeth National Park. It looked like he had sewn this patch on himself; the stitching was erratic and the patch was crooked and seemed to be coming off. His English was not great but everyone in our group was so excited that I didn't want to ruin the mood by asking any questions.

Questions like, "Does anyone else think we are going to die?" Or "Does Coolio have a backup guide? You know, someone to bring up the rear while he is leading the way?"

These important questions remained unspoken as we proceeded herdlike on the path into the gorge.

Coolio began to explain that the canyon rain forest is home to all kinds of wildlife, including the only chimpanzees in the National Park. The area is an important watering source for many animals and is surrounded by savanna.

Through his broken English, he told us we would be hiking to the bottom of the gorge. He also wanted us not to worry about lions because hippos kill way more people in the jungle than lions do. As we came around a steep corner, I took a second glance down the cliff. The canyon fell away from the trail for what seemed like a half mile down. This was going to be a long day.

A mile down the rain-forest path, we hadn't seen a single chimp. I did not want to be the only one to ask Coolio how much longer this hike was going to take, but I knew we were going to have a harder time coming up. I didn't want my fellow safari buddies to think I was like a five-year-old on a road trip asking, "Are we there yet?" But I'd had just about enough— especially when it started to rain.

I was getting seriously tired when one of the men in our group unexpectedly grabbed me. "You don't want to do that," he said as he pulled me back. At first I was indignant. "What? Do what?" I said, slightly annoyed he had startled me. Then I saw it. I had narrowly missed walking face-first into a *huge* spider web. The spider sitting in the middle of the web was the size of a tennis ball, with hairy legs! I just about threw up right then and there.

It wasn't long after the spider o' death incident that we finally hit the floor of the gorge. Our path now ran beside a large, brown river. Coolio suddenly stopped and exclaimed, "Look!" He pointed to the water. The trail was slippery from the downpour, but throwing caution to the wind, we leaned over to check out what Coolio was pointing at. There, just on the edge of the muddy, rushing river was a huge hippo. He swam closer and opened his enormous toothy mouth.

"Remember," Coolio said, "hippos kill more humans than lions kill in the jungle."

"Great! Yeah, thanks, Coolio. We've heard that."

By now I was thinking longingly of and remembering the top of the cliff, feeling like the idiot who has no idea how to get out of this jungle. Finally I said it, in my best super-peppy voice with a huge California smile on my muddy face: "Coolio, how much longer is this hike?"

"You want to go? Follow me," he said. "You are all agreeable to walk across a log for a shortcut?" Everyone nodded in agreement. "Sure," a few voices chimed in. Anything to cut this hike short would be appreciated by all. It was not long before Coolio led us to a colossal tree that had fallen down and was suspended twenty feet above the brown rushing water of the river.

"We can cross this way," he said.

Before this, I had wondered if Coolio was a little crazy. This confirmed the guy was certifiable.

The log was only two feet wide and wet. There was no safety harness, no net or guardrails. But Coolio hopped up and started walking the twenty-five-foot span across the water to the other side. A few of the guys in the group followed him as if this was nothing. I was thinking, *Who do you guys think you are—stunt men?* I personally had not signed up to be on an episode of *Fear Factor.*

But realizing that I was about to be left behind, I hopped onto the wet log and started walking. I knew how to surf and used to race wind surfers in the summer when I was in high school, so I knew my balance was good. But confidence tends to fly out the window when you are in the middle of a jungle, walking on a wet log twenty feet above water that you just saw a huge hippo swimming in. I kept talking to myself: *Just one step in front of the other, Shelene. Soon you will be on dry land.*

Before I knew it, I had made it to the other side. *Whew! Glad that's over.* Before I could kiss the ground, Coolio said, "What's wrong with your friends?"

"What?" I said.

"Your friends." He pointed back across the river to where I had just come from.

There, scared out of their minds, were my roommate, Mary, and my friend Lisa.

I yelled, "Girls! Get your butts over here!"

"No!" they yelled back, adamantly shaking their heads.

"We are afraid of heights," Lisa volunteered.

"And we don't want to slip into the river," Mary added.

"Really?" I yelled back across the river. "So was I. We all were, but this is the only way out. You've just got to do it."

Before Mary and Lisa could respond, Coolio chimed in. "No, no. We can go out the long way, back across the log."

"What?" *Oh, Coolio, I'm going to kill you with your own rusty gun.*

"You mean I didn't need to cross this log and almost die? And now, because of these two chickens, I have to risk my life again to go back across this log?"

I figured Coolio was feeling bad about making me cross back over the log, so I asked him something that had been bugging me since we started this hike.

"And Coolio, let's be honest for a minute. There are no chimps on the chimp hike, are there?"

"Not very often, Momma Shelene," he confessed.

"I knew it!" I said, my hunch confirmed.

"Please follow me," Coolio said.

We made our way back across. Mary decided to take a photo of us walking the log. It's a good thing it wasn't a digital camera. I had to wait to see the pictures until she got home to America and developed them. "Shelene you are not going to believe the shot I got of you crossing the log," she said when she brought the pictures to me.

"Really? Why?"

"Because," she said, holding out the picture for me, "look in the water below you." There in the water directly below me as I was only halfway back across the log for the second time, was a huge crocodile. Oh, my goodness. Talk about freaking out.

Looking back now, I can see that walking across that log was like faith. Everyone in our group told Coolio they would cross the log. As we stood there on one bank of the river we had to cross to get to safety (we thought), the genuineness of our faith was put to the test. It was one thing to watch other people cross over, but it was quite another to put one foot in front of the other twenty feet above a rushing river filled with hippos and crocodiles. It really came down to faith in the log, and not everyone who said they would do it was willing to walk across that log.

———

A few years after my log-walking experience, I read that high-wire-walking legend Nik Wallenda planned to walk a tightrope across the Grand Canyon. Based on my log walk experience, I was feeling the bond with my fellow aerialist. Never mind that my log was only about twenty feet above the water. Nik would be walking across a canyon that was seventy-five times higher than my terrifying twenty-foot exploit.

I told Brice I did not want to miss the excitement of the live television event. So on June 23, 2013, my family and I were glued to the television when Nik crossed the Grand Canyon. He had no net, tether, or safety harness, just a two-inch steel cable stretched between the canyon walls far above the rocky floor. The distance was greater than the height of the Empire State Building.

Nik Wallenda had agreed to wear microphones and to be recorded during the live crossing. Not long after the hazardous event began I was expecting the TV network to bleep out what he was saying—not because it was a swear word or other profanity, but because he was crying out in prayer to his Creator. This is what the microphones picked up: "Praise You, God! Praise You, Jesus! Help me to relax, Lord. . . . You're my King, You're my Protector, You're my Shield, You're my Strength, You're my Lord."

When Nik realized the wire had become slick from blowing dust and the winds had picked up to thirty miles per hour, his prayers intensified. Suddenly the cable began to shake. If he proceeded, it would only continue to get worse. His grandfather had died from a high-wire fall in 1978. That stunt had ended in tragedy when the cable began to shake—just as this cable was shaking now. Nik stopped and crouched down, giving time for the cable to quiet the vibration. "Thank you, Lord. Thank You for calming that cable, God."[1]

One step after another, the twenty-two-minute, fifty-four-second crossing seemed to last an eternity. But as Nik began to draw near to the other side of the canyon he began to run on the wire. The last ten steps were an adrenaline-fueled dash.

When asked later about his prayer on the high wire, he said, "My life is based on my faith. I guess the biggest role that it plays is that if I do fall and die I know where I'm going."[2]

Unlike Nik Wallenda, most of us don't put ourselves in situations that require real faith. You will know you are seeking the face of Jesus when you are so far out of your comfort zone that you can't help but cry out to Jesus as he did fifteen hundred feet above the canyon floor.

But I am not talking about doing high-wire stunts. I am not even talking about low-log stunts. I am talking about seeking Jesus in the place where He said He would be found. I am talking about getting out of your comfort zone, your cultural and social bubble. Getting down and dirty and serving others—because that is where we will see Jesus.

You see, faith is *more* than just believing and saying you believe. Satan himself believes that Jesus Christ was raised from the dead. Satan was there and witnessed the resurrection himself. He believes it happened because he saw it.

"You believe that there is one God. Good! Even the demons believe that—and shudder" (James 2:19).

Just *believing* the right stuff is not enough. True faith is believing and *surrendering* to that belief—to the point that you're willing to step off the edge of safe and sure.

True faith is not just lip service. It's not just "magic words" said in a prayer. It's surrendering to God and allowing the Holy Spirit to invade us and live out love through us.

True faith is offering yourself as a living sacrifice to your Creator and allowing your life to be used for His purposes.

Heavenly Father, I believe in You and in Your trustworthiness and Your perfect track record. I surrender my life to You not just with my words, but with every step I take. Give me the courage to get out of my comfortable bubble and serve others in Your name. Give me the strength to put myself in situations where I need to cry out to You for help. Let Your Holy Spirit invade my heart and live out a life of love through me. Amen.

seven

FREE TO GO

Continue to remember those in prison as if you
were together with them in prison.

—HEBREWS 13:3

I should know by now whenever my friend Julie Hainer and
I get together we will have an unexpected adventure. This day
was no different. My friends Francis and Lisa Chan had invited
me to look at a potential Skip1.org ministry opportunity, and I
had invited Julie because I trusted her uncanny business sense.
The purpose of this trip was to look at a San Francisco Bay
hotel that was in foreclosure. We were exploring the possibility
of putting a group together to buy the hotel and use it for a
prisoner reentry women's home.

Our flight landed and a short time later Francis pulled up
to the airport curb in San Francisco. Julie and I hopped into
the backseat of his van. We expected to see Lisa sitting in the
front passenger seat. Instead, a big burly guy was looking back
at us with a smile. Francis quickly welcomed us. "Hi, guys. We

have had a little change in plans. This is my friend Mario. He is in our two-year program at Project Bayview."

I explained to Julie that Project Bayview is a program that Francis's ministry runs out of a century-old restored commercial building.

"It's a two-year live-in mentoring program to help released prisoners to reenter the community. The downstairs is a restaurant where the ex-cons work and serve food, and the upstairs is a dormitory where mentors and ex-cons live."

Francis explained that Mario had two kids and that police had raided their mom's apartment the night before. She had fled, leaving the two young kids home alone. "I hope you don't mind. We are going to stop and pick up his kids."

I looked at Julie and she gave me a nod with a smile.

"Okay," I said, "we're in!" I knew this day was going to be *nothing* like I had imagined. My well-detailed plans for the day were going to go out the window.

"Mario," Francis said, "tell Shelene and Julie your story and how you got into Project Bayview."

Mario told us he had grown up in Oakland, California. When he was thirteen years old, his mom and dad got busted for running a meth lab out of their house. For Mario, the best thing that came from that was getting to live with his grandma. As nice as that was, by the time he was eighteen, he was growing and selling the best-quality pot in Oakland and was making tons of money. He was making so much money that he taught himself how to make dentures so he could launder the money through the denture company.

Mario went on to explain how he became a world-class cage fighter. The anger stemming from his childhood fueled his passion for violence. In time his drug running caught up with him and he was sentenced to six years in prison, where he became an enforcer because of his cage-fighting experience.

While in prison Mario came to know his Savior, Jesus Christ. After he was released he was accepted into Project Bayview and assigned a mentor. He enrolled in culinary classes and started learning the restaurant trade. He slept on a top bunk at the project, and his mentor slept on the bottom. He had left the old life behind him.

Eight months into his two-year commitment at Project Bayview, Mario received a notice that there was a warrant out for his arrest. He was devastated. It was as if the dark fingers from his old life were reaching up, trying to pull him back into the slime.

Mario went to Francis and Project Bayview director Shawn Gordon for counsel. (You'll hear more about Shawn in chapter 16.)

"What should I do?" he asked. "There is no way I can go back to prison. I just can't go back."

"Mario, you need to turn yourself in," they said.

"But I finally get it now. I have a new life. I just can't go back to prison."

"We understand how you feel, but you are a new man, and as a new man you have to do the right thing and turn yourself in," Shawn said. "God can use your life anywhere. We will pray for you. All the guys will pray for you. But you need to turn yourself in and serve whatever time you are supposed to serve."

"I don't know if I can do that," Mario said.

The next day Francis, Shawn, and some of the guys got together and prayed for Mario as he walked into the police station and turned himself in. It was the weekend, and there was no a judge on the bench, so Mario was locked up in a holding cell. On Monday morning he was transported to the courthouse and ushered into a courtroom before a stern-faced judge. When his case was called, he stood up and took a step forward. "Help me, Jesus," he said under his breath.

"As the judge started reading my rap sheet," Mario told us, "I started thinking back to what I had done in my past life. That list of crimes—it's what I used to take pride in. The longer the better. It's kind of like rich folks, with all their master's degrees and doctorates. But this time as I listened to the judge read my rap sheet, I began to feel sick inside. For the first time in my life I was ashamed."

When the judge finished reading the rap sheet, he said, "Son, do you have anything you'd like to say?"

"Yes, your honor," Mario spoke up in a shaky voice. "There was a time in my life when I took great pride in what you just read about me. But today when I heard that, I am sick. I have a new nature now. There has never been a program the state could offer that could reform me. But I am reformed now. That has been done by my Lord and Savior Jesus Christ. He did that for me."

He paused and looked directly at the judge. "Sir, if God needs me to go back to prison, then I will serve Him there."

The judge stared down at Mario from the bench. There was a long silence. Their eyes met as if the judge were staring down into Mario's soul to see if what he was saying was real.

Abruptly the judge announced, "You know what? I believe you." With that he stamped his documents.

"Son, you are free to go."

Had he heard the judge wrong?

"What? Free to go?" Mario stammered.

"Yes. Free to go. I believe you have changed."

"What?" I repeated, freaking out in the backseat of the car. "Shut up, Mario. That's ridiculous!"

"I know," he said. "When I got back to Bayview, everyone at first thought that I had run and hid out over the weekend. When I told everyone what had happened and I showed them the stamped papers, we all broke down and cried. A bunch of grown men, a bunch of ex-prisoners, standing around crying."

That's what faith does. It replaces the hardest, rockiest hearts with soft, tender ones. It takes a bunch of ex-prisoners who in another life would have killed each other and has them standing in a kitchen crying because God had rescued their brother. Tears of joy because faith had moved a mountain.

When Mario gave his life to Christ, it was crystal clear to him that he had to give up his old life. That life was a disaster, a mess of epic proportion. What God offered Mario was a new life. A totally fresh start. A clean slate. Just as the judge had stamped his paperwork as fulfilled, so Jesus had done for Mario. He had a new life, a new heart. Today, Mario is a single dad working as a chef, doing the right thing, and following Jesus.

The hotel I was exploring with Julie that day did not end up working out, probably because it was only God's excuse to get me to San Francisco to meet Mario. God had so much to teach me through this young man. When we left San Francisco that day, I felt like we had done church. I hadn't entered the doors of a cathedral, sanctuary, or worship center, but once again I had seen Jesus. His presence was all over the smile on the face of an ex-prisoner whose heart had been replaced.

———

In a tiny two-sentence parable in the Bible, Jesus described what it's like to have the new life He wants to give us. "The kingdom of heaven is like treasure hidden in a field. When a man found it, he hid it again, and then in his joy went and sold all he had and bought that field" (Matt. 13:44).

That little story makes me think of the giant treasure room on the Pirates of the Caribbean ride at Disneyland. From the time I was a little child riding on the boats through those dark "caves," I could not wait to see that room. Seeing the piles upon piles of treasure was thrilling to me—huge chests overflowing with golden coins, sparkling gems, gleaming candelabras and shields, and jeweled goblets. This was the kind of hidden treasure I imagine Jesus was talking about in the parable.

In the days before the man discovered the hidden treasure in the field, he did not care about owning this land at all, and he would have laughed at the idea of selling all his possessions to purchase a single piece of land. If somebody had said he had to sell all his possessions and purchase that land he would have been depressed. It would have been an unbearable, ill-advised financial decision. Everything he had worked for would be lost; he would be ruined.

But the treasure changed everything. Suddenly it was "his joy" to sell all he had to buy the land. He could not wait to liquidate everything so he could have rightful title to the secret stash he had stumbled upon.

Finding treasure transformed that man's whole point of view. The possessions that he had held so dear were now meaningless to him—just a means to get the treasure. His priorities changed completely.

Mario's life also changed radically because he found a

treasure. All the money in the world could not compare with the new life Jesus offered him here on earth. The rap sheet that had made him so proud was exposed for the sad, worthless rubbish it was. But even more than that, the promise of eternal life gave him something real and precious he could look forward to.

Mario's pre-Christ life was much more like mine than I thought. Yes, my struggle might not have been so obvious. It didn't involve illicit drugs and violence. My struggle was with putting material possessions before what God has called me do. My struggle was with pride and with the accolades that came with position and awards. I did not have a criminal rap sheet in which I took pride, but I had a list of titles and awards that were just as meaningless and were no more worthy of pride than anything Mario had done.

Charles Spurgeon wrote,

> The temptations of the world are of [a] secret sort to a Christian, though not to the wicked man, for the wicked man sins with his eyes wide open . . . laying hold of iniquity with both his hands, even when destruction stareth him in the face. He will commit a sin that he knows is condemned even by the law of the land: he will rush into a crime, concerning the guilt of which no doubt can be entertained. Not so the Christian: he is taken by secrecy.[1]

When we truly grasp the treasure that we are being offered in an amazing relationship with Jesus Christ, there is no question what we should do. When we truly understand it, we will trade everything we formerly thought was precious to get that treasure. We will want to leave everything behind.

"Then Jesus said to his disciples, 'Whoever wants to be my disciple must deny themselves and take up their cross and follow me. For whoever wants to save their life will lose it, but whoever loses their life for me will find it. What good will it be for someone to gain the whole world, yet forfeit their soul?'" (Matt. 16:24–26).

Are you at a place where you will say, "Whatever it takes, Lord, I will follow and live for You"? Are you willing to waste what this world has to offer for the treasure that Jesus offers you?

Yes, there is a cost to following Jesus when you look at it one way. But in another sense, denying yourself and following Jesus will make you rich beyond your wildest dreams because in doing so you have found the hidden ridiculous treasure.

Lord, I come before You with my hands open wide. It is my joy to say, "Take me, take my abilities, and take all that I have—use it all for Your purpose." Whatever it takes, Lord—I am willing to trade everything for the life You want to give me. Replace my selfish, sinful heart with a heart that has a deep desire for You. Please give me a heart that seeks Your treasure, not the plastic substitute of this world. Give me a heart that breaks at the things that break Your heart. I want a heart that loves others as You love others. With all my love, Lord, with all of myself surrendered, I say amen.

part three

FINDING POWER IN
THE PROMISE

Have you ever thought about what life would be like if you could capture the rush of faith that appears in desperate moments when you cry out to God? A bank robbery, a near-miss auto accident, a cancer diagnosis, or other experience that threatens our lives often results in us crying out to God in faith. What if you could live your entire life with the clarity of split-second faith that crying out to God brings? What if you could seize the force of that faith moment, freeze it in time, and apply it to your everyday life?

I have learned that that kind of ridiculous faith is anchored in our trustworthy God and His amazing commitments to each

of us. Those commitments are promises from an unchanging God—promises that change everything. But not if we don't know them. Not if we fail to believe them and hide them in our hearts. Unwavering confidence in those promises changes uninspired belief into ridiculous faith.

True faith in our trustworthy Creator can mend a broken heart. It can give us hope when we are hopeless and strength when we are weak. It can see our prayers answered. Even a little bit of faith in our absurdly, unbelievably good God can move impossible mountains.

Just watch!

eight

HIDDEN PROMISES

The Lord *is trustworthy in all he promises*
and faithful in all he does.
—Psalm 145:13

Todd Walker was a young man who was turning sixteen. He had grown up in Southern California and came from a well-to-do family. He had come to a point in his life where he had a decision to make about the Christian faith he had been raised with.

About a month before Todd's sixteenth birthday, his dad sat him down and laid it out. "Son, your mom and I have tried to raise you in the right way. We have taught you the things of God since you were a small child. You are going to have to make your relationship with Christ personal or go your own way. That choice is yours, but we pray that you will follow Christ."

Todd was not really sure what he wanted to do with the

whole God thing. As a child he had prayed a prayer to receive Christ and he attended Sunday school because that was what he was "supposed" to do. That was how his parents had raised him. Now there was an inner struggle within his soul. While he appreciated the background and training he had received from the church, frankly, he wanted to experience what else life had to offer.

As time went on he began to get tired of his parents always pushing him about his faith. It was annoying to him and not something he wanted to deal with. He just wanted to live life without being hounded about beliefs.

In the weeks leading up to Todd's sixteenth birthday, his father took him to several car dealerships to test-drive his favorite cars: a brand-new BMW convertible, a blacked-out Camaro muscle car, and a vintage candy-apple-red Corvette. Todd was certain that when his birthday came around in a few weeks he was going to get the car of his dreams from his parents as a birthday present. And why not? They had the money and he was their son. He deserved it.

His dad would not confirm these expectations. But every time he brought up getting a car or what he would be driving, his dad would smile and say, "All I can say is that I promise you will not be disappointed."

Finally the long anticipated day came. Todd's party was amazing, with nearly one hundred of his friends on the grass lawn overlooking the Pacific Ocean, all celebrating *him*. At the end of the party, they sat around, watching him open presents. But there was one present he had his heart set on. It was that one present from his parents he just knew he would get. *How will they do it? Will they blindfold me and lead me to the garage? Will they make a human wall with my friends that will suddenly part?*

When the pile of presents dwindled and then disappeared, he began to wonder: *Aren't they going to reveal it at my party so I can show all my friends?* But the party began to wind down with no gift from his parents, no spectacular reveal.

When all the guests had left, Todd was bewildered. Why hadn't his parents done the reveal? He had wanted to take his friends on a joyride. As he was brooding about it, he heard his mom call: "Todd, can you come into your father's study, honey?" He went into the study and there his parents were with smiles on their faces.

"Son, your mom and I wanted to say happy birthday and give you a small token of our love for you." With that his father pulled a box from behind his back and presented it to his son.

A smile of satisfaction spread across Todd's face. He grabbed the box. *Yes, here it is—the key I have been waiting for all day! What took them so long?* he thought as he tore off the neatly tied ribbon and meticulously folded wrapping paper and threw them to the floor.

The box was larger than he had expected. *How big does a box have to be to hide a key?* He tore off the tape holding the flaps of the box down and then stopped abruptly.

He stared down into the box in pained disbelief, as if an arrow had just been shot through his heart. He could not believe his eyes. There in the bottom of the box was something far different from the key he had been expecting. There between the open cardboard flaps was a beautifully crafted burgundy leather study Bible. Etched in gold on the bottom right corner was his name: Todd Walker.

He was totally silent as he stared down at his name. Then a boiling rage welled up from somewhere deep inside.

"Are you kidding me?" his voice started low but quickly began to build with anger. "A Bible. A *Bible* for my sixteenth birthday? *Really?*"

He stared with venomous hatred at this father. "*You*. You've been trying to shove this stuff down my throat since I was a kid. I'm done with this. Why would you take me to all those dealerships, only to give me a freaking Bible? What kind of sick game are you playing? You have made me look like a fool in front of my friends."

"Son, I—"

Todd raised his hand to cut off his father. "You have all the money in the world and won't share a little with me, your son. I want nothing to do with you." With that he threw the box containing the Bible to the floor and stomped on it, crushing it under his foot. "That's what I think of your stupid God."

He stormed out, leaving his parents standing broken-hearted in stunned silence.

The next few months passed with a considerable icy tension in the house. It was as if something had broken and could not be mended. Although Todd's parents tried to break through and start over, they were met with a growing wall of hatred. Todd came home driving an old motorcycle he had purchased on Craigslist.

Finally Todd's dad put his foot down. They were going to have a family meeting. That's when Todd told them he was moving out. They protested, but he said he was moving in with a friend's parents and there was nothing they could do about it. If they tried to stop him, he would go to court and get a judge to declare him an emancipated minor, free to do what he pleased.

During the next year and a half, Todd lived the kind of life he'd always been curious about. There were lots of girls and parties. And then a phone call.

"Your father's in the hospital, Todd," said his mother. "He's had a heart attack. He wants to see you."

"No thanks," Todd said. "I've seen enough of him for a lifetime."

"At least come meet me at home so we can talk."

"Okay," he relented, "but I have to be somewhere soon."

When Todd got to the house, nobody was home. He let himself in and strolled down the hallway, calling out, "Is anybody home?" Silence. It had been many months since he had been in these halls. To the right he noticed his dad's study. He stepped in. The last time he had been in this room was the day it all began. The day of his sixteenth birthday party. That day seemed like a lifetime ago. So much had changed.

As he wandered around the room inspecting the art, rare books, and various trinkets on the shelves, he noticed a box sitting on a shelf. A corner of the box was crushed on one end. He picked up the box in disbelief. The idiot had kept it—the thing that had come between them. That Bible. It was still in the box he had stomped on the day he stormed out. The day everything had changed.

He peeled back the cardboard flaps, reached in, and pulled out the Bible. Despite a little dust it was still brand-new. The gold-edged pages looked as if they had never been disturbed. He ran his finger over his name. He could smell the fine leather as he turned back the burgundy cover to the pages inside. As he held the book in his hands, it opened to a page where something was tucked between the pages. On the outside of the envelope, he saw his name again, this time in his father's handwriting. *Todd.*

He slowly ran his finger under the flap of the envelope and loosened it. His hands were trembling as he slid a birthday card from the envelope. He opened the card, and something fluttered to the ground. He read the message that had been written two years earlier: "HAPPY SIXTEENTH BIRTHDAY, SON! We hope you enjoy buying the car of your dreams, but may you always let this book drive your life."

He bent down and picked up the paper that had fallen out of the card when he opened it. It was a check for sixty-five thousand dollars with "Sixteenth Birthday Car" written in the memo section.

Todd fell to his knees weeping. "Oh, God," he prayed through his sobs, "I have messed up. I have messed up so badly." He stayed there with his eyes closed, praying and sobbing. He had made such a mess of his life.

When he opened his eyes, there were his father and mother, his dad looking pale and tired. He stood up and rushed into his father's open arms. "I am so sorry. Please, please forgive me," he begged.

"I forgive you," his dad said with a tearful smile on his face.

———

For half of my life, I was too busy doing my own thing to bother with the gifts God had tucked into the pages of the Bible for me. God has hidden something way more valuable than a new dream car in the pages of His Word. It's absolutely full of amazing promises for believers. Ridiculous faith is anchored in our trustworthy and reliable God and the promises He has vowed to fulfill for each of us.

God's promises are commitments from an unchanging God that change everything—but not if we don't know what they are. Not if we fail to find them in those pages, believe them, and hide them in our hearts. We need to have unwavering confidence in those promises, which can change uninspired belief into ridiculous faith.

Sometimes our faith is shallow because we have failed to anchor it in the promises of God. But when we take those promises seriously, our faith grows steady and strong.

His divine power has given us everything we need for a godly life through our knowledge of him who called us by his own glory and goodness. Through these he has given us his *very great and precious promises, so that through them you may participate in the divine nature,* having escaped the corruption in the world caused by evil desires. (2 Peter 1:3–4, emphasis added)

God teaches here that liberation from our own faults and failures and the ability to experience God's very nature come from knowing and trusting His precious and very great promises. God is a promise maker and He is a promise keeper. His promises are commitments that will not be broken. They are guarantees and can be relied on forever.

Following are just some of God's promises to those who are His:

- I will never leave or forsake you. (Deut. 31:6)
- I will pursue you with goodness and mercy. (Ps. 23:6)
- I will show you how to live and keep watch over you. (Ps. 32:8)
- I will be with you and make you stronger. (Isa. 41:10)
- I will renew your strength when you depend on Me. Your energy will not give out. (Isa. 40:31)
- If you stick close to Me, you will lead a fruitful life. (John 15:5–7)
- I will give you words that you need to speak. (Luke 12:12)
- I will not let you be tempted beyond what you can bear. (1 Cor. 10:13)
- I will give you wisdom for every new challenge. (James 1:5)
- I will give you peace when you practice what I teach you. (Phil. 4:9)
- I will take care of all your needs. (Phil. 4:19)
- I will prepare a heavenly place for you so you can be with Me. (John 14:2–3)
- I will take good care of your future. (Prov. 16:9)
- I am always there to help when you need Me. (Ps. 46:1–3)
- I will rescue you from your own faults. (Rom. 10:9–10)
- I will not allow anything to separate you from My love. (Rom. 8:38–39)

The above verses are paraphrased. I have listed these verses in their full text in the appendix. I hope you will read them, memorize them, hide them in the recesses of your mind, and hold them dear to your heart. They will serve as an unshakable anchor to your own ridiculous faith.

Some people might say, "Shelene, what about cancer, losing my job, or the death of innocent children? Where are God's promises in those things?"

Let's face it—yes, godly people have died young. Some very strong Christians have become martyrs *because* of their faith. Does that mean God is unfaithful and His promises untrustworthy? Not at all.

From God's perspective, life extends beyond the grave, and His promises hold true for eternity. Sometimes God will grant physical protection and deliverance to His children in this world. But even if He allows some to suffer, in the unseen world their journey continues and their life abounds. They are freed from the pain, sorrow, and suffering that was the result of sin coming into this world, and they see God's promises fully fulfilled.

Jesus' disciples viewed God's own Son being nailed to a cross as the worst calamity of all. But God had a plan. Now in hindsight we can see that what was then viewed as disaster— Jesus' death—was actually God's wonderful provision for all humanity to get to God. That is a message so beautiful that the most heinous instrument for capital punishment ever devised, the cross, adorns our churches and our homes and is worn around our necks. It's all about trusting our amazing God, who sees the big picture that we won't understand until the day we stand before Him and finally say, "Ahh, that's why."

God, as I reflect on the amazing promises You have made to me, I am overwhelmed. I cannot help but to think about all my faults. I am so ashamed that my faint heart constantly forgets who You are and Your steadfast faithfulness. When I am weak, help me to remember the commitments You have made to me. Help me to rely on Your trustworthy nature. Give me the strength to remember Your pure words of truth that will sustain my faith and my very life. Thank You for the undeserved favor You have shown me. Amen.

nine

NATURALLY NOAH

Promise: "I will be with you and and help you and make you stronger."

By faith Noah, when warned about things not yet seen, in holy fear built an ark to save his family. By his faith he condemned the world and became heir of the righteousness that is in keeping with faith.
—HEBREWS 11:7

When I was pregnant with our first child, Blake, not more

than a few months in, I began to get a nesting feeling. This was a new experience for me. I have never been one who is overly excited about crafts, scrapbooking, or decorating. I truly appreciate those who have talent in these areas and wish I were more artistically inclined, but such activities have never been my thing. So I figured I would embrace the inexplicable feelings of creativity I was experiencing for the first time in my life and take on an interior decorating project: the nursery. I knew I needed to get Brice on board, so I decided to have a conversation with him about the second bedroom we had designated as the baby's room. It went something like this:

"Brice, I've been thinking. We need to get the nursery set up for the baby."

"What do you have in mind?"

"Well, to start, I thought we could go shopping for a crib."

"Yes, honey, but I thought that was something you might want to do with your sister. Besides, we have lots of time, like seven months' worth of time."

"Honey, we don't know that. What if the baby comes early?"

"Really, Shelene?"

"What? I just want to be prepared."

Not wanting to upset a pregnant woman, he relented. "Maybe we could go look this weekend, but we don't need to buy anything just yet."

With my pregnant nesting hormones kicking in, I began counting the days. When Saturday rolled around, remembering that the first "let's redecorate and make a nursery" conversation had not gone so well, I decided to take a more subtle approach.

Inviting Brice to follow me into the garage, I simply took the keys to the car, jumped into the driver's seat, and motioned to the passenger's seat as he got in.

"Where are we going?" he asked.

"I thought we might look at some baby furniture."

I made the short drive to the baby store and pulled up with a screech. I had waited to come here for nearly a week.

We parked and went in. We didn't know it, but we each had a large red-ink stamp on our foreheads that said SUCKER.

The saleswoman greeted us with a fake smile, in a sappy-sweet "I want all your money" sort of way. We explained we were going to have a baby, and she broke into a well-rehearsed line about how she never would have guessed I was pregnant.

Really, lady, this is a baby store. Virtually everybody shopping in here is pregnant. I wondered how many hundreds of times she had used that line.

She immediately escorted us to the most expensive suite of baby furniture in the store. The luxuriously varnished matching set included a handcrafted crib, a changing table, a dresser, and a rocker-ottoman combo. The plush bedding depicted the cutest little Noah's ark scene. A happy gray-bearded Noah was corralling a sweet lion, hippo, and giraffe.

I began to ooh and ah over this ensemble until Brice asked the question, "How much for everything?"

I was quite proud of him for getting into the baby shopping spirit and stood there simply admiring him for a second. Admiring him just long enough for the enthusiastic saleslady to do exactly what my husband had requested and tell us out loud the price for everything.

Didn't she know Sales 101? You *never* ever, *ever* give the combined price for everything. What was she thinking?

As she stated the price, the entire room seemed to change into a slow-motion scene from a movie. The look on Brice's face went frame-by-frame from happy bliss to one of shock and horror and then finally to unadulterated terror.

After a minute, the shockwave having somewhat settled,

he calmly asked, "Do you have any other cribs we can see?" Although he was outwardly calm, cool, and collected, the way his voice cracked when he said "other cribs" provided me a dead giveaway as to where he was coming from.

She proceeded to take us away from the well-lit centerpiece display to a dark part at the back of the store. She pointed to a line of cribs that included the assemble-yourself types constructed with cheaply manufactured particle board and plastic fittings. I could tell that the prices of these ragtag specimens were more to Brice's liking but that after seeing the quality of the first set, he would have a hard time settling for these poor excuses for cribs for his firstborn child. At this point I was beginning to regain some respect for the salesperson's abilities. *Show 'em the best first and they won't like anything else. Nice.*

Then the saleswoman really poured it on. "I know it's seven months and all before the baby comes, but you should be aware it takes up to six months just to receive and fulfill the orders. So you really don't want to wait. If you do, you probably won't be able to get what you want."

"Can't we just buy the floor model?" I asked.

"No, we don't sell the floor models since that's what we use to show their excellent quality." She said it with a smug, satisfied smile, as if she was so proud of herself for overcoming my objection.

"Honey, all we really need to do is put everything on order," I said to Brice. "I'm having a baby shower, and we can probably have everyone pitch in to pay for these extras."

"Do we really need all this stuff?" Brice asked. "Honestly, won't we only use it for a year or so? Why can't we use the crib to change the baby? The side drops down, right?"

It took some convincing, but eventually Brice saw the wisdom in ordering the entire suite of furniture. I said things like, "We can use this same set for all our kids," and the salesperson said things like, "We will give you a 10 percent discount on everything if you order them all today."

She had picked up on the fact that we were double-teaming Brice, and he was about to go down. Then she added the final blow. "And if you do it today, we will throw in the bedding for free."

"What's the bedding?" Brice asked wearily.

"Do you see all the soft items with the Noah's ark print? That's the "Naturally Noah" set. The comforter, the pillows, the crib skirt, the mattress. None of those are included in the price I gave you."

"Of course they aren't. So it's basically unusable without Naturally Noah," Brice said in a tone that made it clear he was just going to give up. "Shelene, if you want it put it on order, go ahead."

That's how Noah came to live in our home—a smiley, cute old man with a white beard on a cute little wooden boat with some happy animals. That's what I had always thought the story of Noah was about anyway. I had held this picture in my head since childhood and looking at the walls in my nursery just reinforced that image.

Then I decided to read the Bible through in one year. I started at Genesis 1:1 and began to read a few chapters a day. When I began reading the story of Noah, I was absolutely horrified.

The story of Noah in the Bible is not really an appropriate children's story. It's a story about wickedness and evil. It's a gruesome story about death and destruction. About God's ultimate judgment of evil.

When I finished reading the story of Noah, I called Brice in astonishment.

"Honey, have you ever read the story of Noah's ark?"

"Yes."

"It's crazy! I can't believe we put that all over our nursery. It's about death, dying, and destruction."

"Yes, that's true, but the story also tells us a lot about Noah's faith. Noah spent something like 120 years building the ark without ever having seen rain."

I will never forget that conversation. The Naturally Noah crib was long ago given to another young couple, and our kids are now teenagers, but I will always remember that image of the cute, white-haired smiling man—and the shock of realizing the real story was so much more than that.

REAL FAITH BELIEVES GOD

The real Noah's faith was astounding. God told Noah that He would flood the earth, and Noah believed it, demonstrating his faith. *Real faith believes God.* Not only did Noah believe God; he believed God so deeply and so fervently that he changed everything in his life to do what God asked. I find it fascinating that many Bible scholars believe that up until the flood, it had never rained on the earth, and the atmosphere was like a cloudy mist. Think about that for a minute. Think about the faith it took for Noah to prepare for a flood when it was quite possible he had never even seen rain.

Imagine if I came to you and told you that it is going to farg.

"What the heck does farg mean?" you would ask.

"I know you have never seen farg before and you've never heard of it, but trust me, you need to dedicate the rest of your life to building a shelter so that when it does farg, you will be saved."

Now you might go along with me for a while, perhaps a few weeks or a couple of months or, if you really like me, maybe even a year. But after a few years with no farg attack, I am pretty sure you would give up. I know I would.

Not Noah. Despite never having seen rain in his lifetime, despite the certain ridicule of his neighbors, he dropped everything and spent 120 years building a giant boat. He did not stop after a few years; he didn't even stop after 50 or 80 years. Because he was full of faith, Noah took God at His word and completed his building project.

The reality is, we are all building something. We are either building a life for now or a life for later. Noah chose to live a life for later, and because of that pursuit he saved his entire family and every animal on the planet.

The choice to live a life of faith ensures that you will endure the ridicule of your friends, neighbors, and community. But take solace in the fact that the majority is almost never right. The wide road leads to destruction, and the narrow road leads to what is right. What most people don't realize is that if we follow Noah's example and start building something God has set out for us to do, we will encounter more peace and fulfillment than any earthly success can offer.

REAL FAITH PROMPTS ACTION

The other thing that was amazing about Noah is that his belief prompted serious action. I mean he *really* worked on the ark. Can you imagine the intensive manual labor it took to make an ark that was the size of a modern ship—437.50 feet long, 72.92 feet wide, and 4 stories high, *all by hand* (Gen. 6:15)? If you turned the ark on one end, it would stand as tall as a forty-story building. All that was built by one guy and his family, and that is without the materials being readily available. Noah had to be his own logger, logging mill, hauler, and pitch maker. That is action.

R. C. Sproul wrote,

> At its root, this is what faith is. It is not believing *in* God. It's believing *God*. The Christian life is about believing God. . . . It is about following Him into places where we've never been, into situations that we've never experienced, into countries that we've never seen—because we know who He is.[1]

I've been known to complain about spending two hours painting on a mission's trip. That's pretty pathetic when compared to how long Noah kept at it. Yes, I could learn a lot from Noah. The bottom line is, I really appreciate Noah's amazing example of work ethic and perseverance for the assignment God gave him—all based on his simple belief that what God said was true. Real faith prompts action.

BY FAITH NOAH WAS CALLED RIGHTEOUS

The most important aspect of Noah's story has to do with faith that made him righteous despite his imperfections. Hebrews 11:7 says that Noah "became an heir of the righteousness that comes by faith" (ESV).

This is a truth we all need to know, believe, and live out in our individual relationships with God: righteousness comes by faith. Whether the first time you have thought about God is the day you opened the pages of this book or you've had a deep, long-term relationship with Him, we all need to understand that faith is our path to our Father.

"For it is by grace you have been saved, through faith— and this is not from yourselves, it is the gift of God—not by works, so that no one can boast. For we are God's handiwork, created in Christ Jesus to do good works, which God prepared in advance for us to do" (Eph. 2:8–10).

The reason Noah was spared was because he "found favor [grace] in the eyes of the Lord" (Gen. 6:8). Just as we do now through Christ Jesus.

God, grant me the faith to believe what You say in Your Word and empower me to live a life of action motivated by that belief. Remind me that You will be with me to strengthen and help me when I am weary and when those around me mock my faith. Thank You, Lord, for the undeserved favor You have shown me. I pray Your amazing gift of grace will motivate me to live a life of action for You. Amen.

ten

THE HANDS OF GOD

Promise: "I will pursue you with
goodness and mercy."

. . . who through faith conquered kingdoms,
administered justice, and gained what was
promised; who shut the mouths of lions. . . .
—HEBREWS 11:33

Several years ago, along with our church's media team, I
was coproducing and hosting *What's Your Story?*, a cable
TV program. This show about inspiring stories in the lives of
everyday people always started the same way. With our mobile
film crew standing by, we would bring out the rather large
church phone book. I would close my eyes and start flipping the
pages. As the pages fanned by, I would randomly stick my finger on one of the four thousand names the directory contained.
On this particular day, my finger landed on Bruce and

Jaimie Watson. I was vaguely familiar with Bruce and Jaimie. They were a twenty-something couple I had first met when they were volunteering with the midweek children's Awana program. Cameras rolling, I dialed the phone number.

"Hello." A woman's voice answered.

"Hi, Jaimie. It's Shelene Bryan from Cornerstone Church."

"Oh, hi, Shelene."

"This may sound strange, but we do this show called *What's Your Story?* We randomly pick people from the church directory to be interviewed."

"Yes, yes, I've seen it. I love the show!"

"Well, today my finger landed on you and Bruce. Are you guys available right now for our crew to come to your house and ask you a few questions?"

"Right now?" she asked hesitantly. I could tell the timing was not so good. (Of course, this was a totally understandable response to the "Hi, can we invade your privacy and film you in the next five minutes so two hundred thousand people can see you forever" phone call—but no matter, we had a show to produce and a story to get.)

"Yes, right now. It will probably only take an hour or so," I said.

"Oh my gosh, really, *wow*, well . . . okay, what the heck. Come on over!" she said.

"Okay, we'll be right there."

I hung up the phone. "Woohoo, let's go!"

We piled into the vans, and fifteen minutes later the crew was setting up in the Watsons' living room. During that interview I heard their story for the first time—part one of an amazing work God wanted to do in the lives of this couple.

Bruce and Jaimie were college sweethearts. They met at The Master's College in Southern California, where Bruce, a high school basketball star, was attending on a full-ride basketball scholarship. They discovered they both enjoyed the game of basketball and the Los Angeles Lakers in particular. Building on that connection, they fell in love and soon were married.

Bruce and Jaimie were enjoying the beauty of young love and getting used to the ups and downs the first year of marriage can bring. They planned to wait a few years before starting a family so they could settle into their careers. But less than a year into their newlywed bliss, Jaimie became pregnant. Although the news was unexpected, Jaimie and Bruce were thrilled about it. They let their families know and began celebrating the miracle of the growing child in Jaimie's tummy.

Within a few weeks it was time for Jaimie's first checkup with the OBGYN. After signing her life away on a mountain of papers—"new patient paperwork," it was apologetically explained—the nurse called her back to an examining room and handed Jaimie a paper gown that looked like a giant bib slit entirely up both sides. This thing was supposed to be held together by two tiny strings that did not cooperate. It's so wonderful to meet your doctor for the first time wearing a slit paper toga for an outfit.

She was told the doctor would be "right in."

So there she was, sitting on the edge of the Naugahyde examining table in her paper toga, waiting and waiting.

Turns out, "right in" in nurse-speak meant thirty-five minutes later. Eventually, though, the doctor entered the little examining room.

"Hi, I'm Dr. Hansen," he said, extending his hand in an awkward greeting.

Jaimie shook his hand and explained that she had taken a pregnancy test at her family doctor's office and it had come back positive.

"Let's take a look," he said. "You should probably be about six or seven weeks along, so we should be able to hear the baby's heartbeat today."

Some sort of listening contraption was brought in. The doctor smeared some gel on Jaimie's abdomen and began swirling what looked like a wand around, around, and around.

Nothing.

After a few minutes of repeating this process to no avail, Dr. Hansen said nonchalantly, "Well . . . sometimes we can't hear a heartbeat at this stage—no matter. Let me bring in the nurse and we can do an ultrasound."

A few minutes later the nurse came in and hooked Jaimie up to another contraption that she explained was an ultrasound machine. Another wand was swirled around on Jaimie's tummy as the nurse looked intently at a small screen. After a few minutes of examination, the nurse looked stressed. After another few minutes of the repeated circle movements, Jaimie could tell something was wrong.

The nurse finally stopped. "Umm," she said nervously, "I'd better get the doctor. I'll be right back."

"Is everything all right?" Jaimie asked, as a feeling of dread began to creep over her.

The nurse put on a superficial smile. "Oh, sure. You're going to be just fine." She awkwardly stepped backward and then scurried out the examining room door, closing it tightly behind her.

That was evasive, Jaimie thought. *"You're going to be just fine"? What about my baby?*

Her mind began to race. *What is going on? Where is the doctor?*

A few minutes later Dr. Hansen reentered the room with a solemn look on his face.

"Mrs. Watson, I'm sorry to tell you this, but . . . you've had a miscarriage."

Those words hit like a ton of bricks.

What? How can that be? Jaimie thought.

"You can tell that from the ultrasound?" she asked.

"Well, to be frank, we simply can't find anything on the ultrasound," he said. "I went back to my office to check your urine sample to make sure we had the right diagnosis, and you did have numbers indicating you were in fact pregnant. At this point we are going to need to do a dilation and curettage, commonly called a D & C."

Jaimie had no idea what a D & C was, but it certainly did not sound good.

"But I don't have any signs of a miscarriage—no bleeding, no cramping, I feel fine."

"I understand, but we are going to need you to come in on Friday to perform the procedure on you." The doctor explained that a D & C involved scraping the uterine walls to make sure no tissue was left behind to become infected.

"Uhhh, okay," Jaimie said, overwhelmed.

She called Bruce and told him what was happening. They made plans for her D & C.

Two days later, on Friday, Bruce took Jaimie to her appointment. As she was changing from her clothes into a hospital gown, she began to have a feeling that something was wrong.

"God, please help me through this," she prayed. "Please guide the hand of the doctor."

A few minutes later she was ushered back to a cold white room that looked like an operating room.

Doctor Hansen explained she would be awake in what they described as "twilight." She would not be fully knocked out, but she would not be able to feel anything. As the nurse put the "twilight" drug into her IV, a haze came over her.

Jaimie began to hear a whirring sound—like a vacuum. The sucking it made reminded her of the sound a pool vacuum made when sucking up everything in its path. Eventually the sucking sound stopped, and an eerie silence fell over the room. As the drugs began to wear off, Bruce came in to see Jaimie and to speak with the doctor.

"Everything went very well," Dr. Hansen said. "Jaimie should not have any cramping because I took extra time to clean everything out."

"Okay, thank you, Doctor," Bruce said.

Within a few hours Bruce took Jaimie home, and just as the doctor had advised, she took it easy for a few days. Bruce and Jaimie spent that time together mourning the loss of the unborn child. But a week after the procedure, Jaimie confided in her mom. "You know, Mom, it's really strange, but I feel more pregnant than ever."

"Jaimie, honey, you've been pregnant for a couple of months, and it takes time for your hormones to get back to normal."

"That's probably it," Jaimie said.

About a week after her D & C, Jaimie was startled awake at six in the morning by a phone call.

She groggily picked up the phone. "Hello?"

"Hello, Ms. Watson?" an efficient sounding voice on the other end of the line asked.

"Yes."

"This is Dr. Hansen. How are you feeling?"

"I feel okay."

"Are you in any pain?"

"No, I'm not in any pain," Jaimie answered cautiously. "Why? Is there something wrong?"

"Are you sure you're not in pain?"

"*Yes*, I'm absolutely sure," she insisted.

"Mrs. Watson, remember how I told you that we routinely send the D & C tissue samples to the lab to be sure we got all the fetal material?"

"Yes."

"I just got word from the lab that no fetal tissue was found."

"What does that mean?" Jaimie asked.

"It means that you must have an ectopic pregnancy and the baby is implanted outside the uterus, probably in the fallopian tubes, and that's quite dangerous. I need you to get to the hospital right away for emergency surgery. And have someone drive you."

"Okay," she said, "I'll leave just as soon as I can."

"Mrs. Watson, I'm serious. You need to get to the hospital—*now*. I called you this early because I wanted to be sure you do not have anything to eat or drink. I have called ahead, and the doctors are waiting for you."

Jaimie hung up the phone.

God, why are You doing this? she thought as she turned to tell Bruce the news.

———

Fifteen minutes later, Jaimie was being rushed to the hospital. When she arrived she was whisked into an emergency room with curtains for walls.

The ER doctor walked in and introduced himself. "We have been called by your doctor. I understand you have an ectopic pregnancy. Let's see what's going on."

He hooked Jaimie up to the now familiar ultrasound machine. After a few minutes with the wand, he said, "Excuse me, I'll be back shortly."

A few minutes later he reappeared with another doctor, who looked intently at the screen for what seemed like several minutes.

The two doctors began talking excitedly and finally said that they wanted to get Dr. Hansen on the phone.

"Okay," Jaimie said.

Finally, the ER doctor reentered Jaimie's room and sat down next to the hospital bed. "Mrs. Watson, I don't know how to tell you this."

Oh no. Do I have cancer? she thought. "Tell me what?"

"It's . . . well . . . it's your baby."

"What baby? I don't have a baby—at least not since the D & C," Jaimie told him.

"That's what I have been told, but . . . well, I don't quite understand this, especially given that you supposedly had a D

& C. But Mrs. Watson, your baby is right there in the womb, right where it should be."

"What . . . what are you saying?"

"I am saying you are still pregnant with what looks like a normal pregnancy, with your baby right where it belongs."

"How can that be?" Jaimie said. "I thought the D & C would have sucked out everything."

"It should have. There is no medical explanation for this, and I certainly don't understand it," the doctor said with tears in his eyes. "All I can say is—it's a miracle! It's the hands of God."

After composing herself, Jaimie put her clothes back on. She headed out to the ER waiting room, where her mom was waiting.

"You are white as a ghost. What's going on, Jaimie? Why are you out here? I thought you were having surgery?"

"No, Mom. I'm pregnant," Jaimie said with a huge smile on her face.

"*What?* Honey, how can that be?"

"It's a miracle, Mom. It's the hands of God!"

Seven months later a beautiful, healthy little girl, Sabrina Watson, was born.

———

"Stop the cameras!" I said. Tears were streaming from my eyes, smearing my on-camera makeup all over my face, but I didn't care. When we had set out earlier that morning to do another episode of *What's Your Story?* I had not imagined I would hear such an amazing testimony of God's faithfulness.

I dried my face and I gave Jaimie a big hug. "Oh my gosh,

thank you for sharing this! I never knew what a miracle God did in your life."

As I have reflected on this miracle, a picture of God's hands reaching into the womb and surrounding tiny, precious Sabrina comes to mind. The Creator's grip cupped around His precious child, protecting her from the suction of that vacuum hose. Hands protecting His little girl.

> *For you created my inmost being;*
> *you knit me together in my mother's womb.*
> (Ps. 139:13)

It would not be the first time that protective hands kept safe a beloved child. In Hebrews 11:32–33, the Bible describes the heroic faith of Daniel and how protective hands shut the mouths of hungry lions. "And what more shall I say? I do not have time to tell about . . . the prophets, who through faith . . . shut the mouths of lions."

The story of Daniel in the lions' den is one of the most iconic stories in the Bible. Most people think they know it well, and so did I. But after studying this story anew, I was shocked about the misconceptions I had held since childhood.

First, Daniel was not a young man at the time he was thrown into the lions' den. I'm quite sure the felt figures that my Sunday school teacher put up on the felt background showed Daniel as a young, handsome figure in a white and brown robe and King Darius as an ancient man with a white beard. He always seemed to me like a fatherly figure to Daniel.

I was shocked to learn that Daniel was actually about eighty years old when he was thrown to the lions and that

King Darius was not a fatherly figure at all. Daniel was more like an elder statesman whom Darius relied upon. Darius was sixty-two when he took over ruling Babylon for the Medo-Persian Empire. It's more probable that Darius loved Daniel as a dad, rather than the other way around.

Not everyone loved Daniel, though. There was a group of men in Babylon who hated him because he constantly demonstrated his unwavering faith in God.

Daniel would go to his room, open his window, and pray to God three times every day. This was something he did like clockwork and everybody knew it. So Daniel's enemies decided to use that practice to lay a trap.

They convinced King Darius to sign a decree preventing prayer to anyone but himself. Despite the penalty of certain death, Daniel continued to open his window and get down on his knees and pray to his heavenly Father.

The men went as a group to King Darius and said to him, "Remember, Your Majesty, that according to the law of the Medes and Persians no decree or edict that the king issues can be changed."

This was devastating for King Darius, who tried to undo the law but could not.

. . . So the king gave the order, and they brought Daniel and threw him into the lions' den. . . . Then the king returned to his palace and spent the night without eating and without any entertainment being brought to him. And he could not sleep.

At the first light of dawn, the king got up and hurried

to the lions' den. When he came near the den, he called to Daniel in an anguished voice, "Daniel, servant of the living God, has your God, whom you serve continually, been able to rescue you from the lions?"

Daniel answered, "May the king live forever! My God sent his angel, and he shut the mouths of the lions. They have not hurt me, because I was found innocent in his sight. Nor have I ever done any wrong before you, Your Majesty."

The king was overjoyed and gave orders to lift Daniel out of the den. And when Daniel was lifted from the den, no wound was found on him, because he had trusted in his God. (Dan. 6:15–16, 18–23)

In the past, whenever I heard this story, I always tried to explain away God's part in shutting the mouths of the lions. I would say things like, "Daniel was sure lucky those lions had just had a big meal, or he would have been dinner." But then, when I reread the account, I was shocked at the description that these lions were famished:

At the king's command, the men who had falsely accused Daniel were brought in and thrown into the lions' den, along with their wives and children. And before they reached the floor of the den, the lions overpowered them and crushed all their bones. (Dan. 6:24)

The story of Daniel is an amazing story of God's faithfulness. Daniel had risked everything to meet God in prayer, and God did not leave him hanging. He was there, ready to rescue Daniel in the craziest, most ridiculous way. Of course,

God could have nixed the whole lions' den scenario way back when the men were plotting against Daniel. He could have had Daniel's enemies choke on a date or get run over by a speeding chariot. Or he could have had Darius figure out a legal exception. There are always legal loopholes—just ask my husband.

Any one of a hundred scenarios could have saved Daniel a whole lot of stress. But clearly there was something about Daniel's having to go through the journey. Something God wanted Daniel to learn about His faithfulness.

Sometimes we get so caught up in the horrific stress of lions' den moments that we forget God is always bigger than our circumstances. We forget God has allowed those particular circumstances—no matter how horrible and impossible they seem—to teach us something.

Let's face it, there are not too many circumstances we will face that are more horrible and impossible than the prospect of being torn limb from limb by a pack of hungry lions. I would have bet against Daniel ever coming out of that den of ferocious, starving predators. Yet the Lord's hands sealed their hungry mouths shut and nothing harmed him.

I would have bet against little Sabrina Watson ever surviving the procedure. Yet the faithful hands of God sealed the end of that vacuum.

Sometimes it's just the faithful hands of God that rescue us for no other reason than that He can and He is faithful. That is the kind of God we are called to serve, a ridiculously faithful God in whom we can have ridiculous faith.

God, thank You for rescuing me from situations I am not even aware of. Thank You for being faithful to me when

I am faithless and clueless. Help me to trust Your goodness and mercy even in circumstances I do not understand. Give me the strength and faith to live a life worthy of my undeserved rescue. Amen.

eleven

MESSAGE IN A BLANKET

Promise: "I will carefully establish your steps."

> *And by faith even Sarah, who was past childbearing age, was enabled to bear children because she considered him faithful who had made the promise. And so from this one man, and he as good as dead, came descendants as numerous as the stars in the sky and as countless as the sand on the seashore.*
> —HEBREWS 11:11–12

Sabrina Watson's rescue by the protective hands of God was a miracle that Bruce and Jaimie Watson would think about every single day as their daughter grew from a beautiful baby into a strong, healthy, athletic child. But God was not yet finished with the Watson family. Not even close.

Just after Sabrina's fifth birthday, Bruce and Jaimie

decided it was time to have another child. This had always been Jaimie's plan, to have their second child after their first was off to school.

But as the months turned into years with no pregnancy, Jaimie began to wonder what God was doing.

"Lord," she prayed, "what's going on here? I know You want us to have another child."

Jaimie felt it was time to visit her doctor and have some tests done. After a battery of testing, everything came back normal. There was no reason she should not be able to get pregnant. The doctor suggested, "It might be your husband. Maybe he should be tested."

Jaimie and Bruce decided to make an appointment with the renowned fertility specialists at UCLA. When all the test results were in, the doctor asked to meet with the Watsons. "Bruce, I understand you were concerned about a possible low sperm count. Well, you don't have a low sperm count; you have a no-sperm count."

"*None?*" Bruce asked, shocked. "How can that be? My wife and I have a daughter."

"Yes, we have a five-year-old daughter," Jaimie confirmed.

The doctor looked at Jaimie. "Not with this man. That's medically impossible."

"Excuse me?" Jaimie said. "Sir, Bruce is my husband. He's the only man I've ever slept with or will ever sleep with, and I'm going to leave it at that."

"Well, then," the doctor said, seeing he had touched a nerve, "all I can say is that was a one-in-a-million chance, and you two most likely will never have another child."

Jaimie was devastated by this news. All their careful plans seemed to be unraveling.

What she didn't realize at the time was that God had a different plan. A more perfect plan.

As Sabrina's sixth, seventh, and then eighth birthdays passed with no pregnancy, one of Jaimie's close friends brought up adoption.

"I don't want to adopt," Jaimie explained to her friend. "I want my own biological children. I want a little boy who looks like Bruce since we already have a girl who looks like me."

A few days after Jaimie uttered those words to her friend, our pastor started talking a lot about "true religion." He said that true religion was taking care of widows and orphans. Some days Bruce would say, "Jaimie, we should adopt," but Jaimie was against it. Then other times Jaimie would say something like, "Maybe we should look into adopting," and Bruce would say no. She knew in her heart she was supposed to have another child, so she decided to pray.

"God, I know Sabrina was a miracle, I know You protected her, and I know it's too much to ask for another miracle. But I am asking for one anyway. And I pray for Your wisdom on what to do."

After praying, Jaimie got a very strong sense in her heart that she was fighting God. *I have to quit doing that,* she thought. A few days later she prayed, "Okay, Lord, whatever You want we will do, but please confirm for us that it is really what You want."

Still with serious doubts in their minds, Jaimie and Bruce contacted an international adoption agency and had an informational meeting. Despite their continued uncertainty, they agreed to move forward in the process. Because they were required to pick a source country, they picked Ethiopia—for no particular reason. Jaimie could not even find it on a map.

As Jaimie filled out mounds and mounds of paperwork, she quietly begged God to prepare her heart to love whatever child He had for her. "Lord, if You want us to adopt, erase my doubt and give me a child I can love as much as I love Sabrina."

Then one day Sabrina was feeling off and asked her mom if she could stay home from school.

"Well, okay, honey, but I don't want you to get too far behind."

Midmorning that day, Jaimie received a call from a number she did not recognize. The area code was the same as the adoption agency headquarters.

"Hello."

"Yes, hi. Mrs. Watson?"

"Yes, this is Jaimie Watson."

"This is Laura from the New Hope adoption agency."

"Oh, yes. Hi, Laura," Jaimie said warmly.

"I wanted to let you know we got a referral this morning for an infant baby boy from Ethiopia."

"Oh my gosh, really?" Jaimie said, not really sure what to think.

"He is about twenty days old, the youngest referral we have ever had. He was left to be found. I am going to e-mail you some pictures."

Stunned and not sure how to react, Jaimie said, "Okay. I'll look at the pictures, thank you." She hung up the phone and told Sabrina what had just happened.

"Call Dad and have him come home so we can all look at the pictures together," Sabrina said.

"Good idea." Jaimie punched the keypad on her phone.

"Bruce, you've got to come home immediately," she insisted. She quickly explained the call and the pictures waiting in her in-box.

"Okay, I'll be there in about a half hour," he said. "And Jaimie, don't open anything until I get there. I know you."

Jaimie and Sabrina paced around the house like caged animals until Bruce got home.

"What took so long?"

"I told you a half hour—goodness. I got here in less than that. Let's go open the e-mail."

Bruce sat down at their desktop computer, and Jaimie and Sabrina crowded around, looking over his shoulder.

He sorted through a long list of recent e-mails. "This is it!" He held the mouse over the e-mail with an attachment icon.

Click!

What they saw next was an image that burned itself into their hearts. The picture was of a tiny baby boy wrapped in a blanket. He looked thin and perhaps a little sickly. The e-mail said his name was Teggie. As Jaimie's eyes tracked down the photograph from Teggie's face to his little body, suddenly she felt as if she had been hit by lightning.

"Bruce, zoom in on that blanket!"

"What?" he asked in confusion.

"The blanket—zoom in on the blanket!"

As the image grew with the slide of the mouse, Bruce's jaw dropped in disbelief.

The baby's little body was wrapped in a blanket, but it was

not just any baby blanket. It sported the familiar purple and gold logo of their favorite basketball team.

"He's . . . he's in a Lakers blanket!" Jaimie blurted out.

In that instant Bruce and Jaimie knew without a single doubt that this tiny baby was their little son.

"It's our son! Undeniably our son," Bruce said with a joyful laugh.

They were all crying now. They hugged and then held hands, and Bruce prayed. "God, thank You for this boy. We no longer have any doubt that he is our son. We are so grateful for Your faithfulness."

How that Los Angeles Lakers blanket made it all the way around the world and then found its way around this little baby who was left to be found, and how now a photograph of this little newborn had found its way into the in-box of the Laker-crazy Watson family in Los Angeles, California, only God will ever know.

It's what I like to call *ridiculous*.

THE EVIDENCE OF GOD'S UNSEEN HANDS

Faith is "evidence" of what we can't see. Evidence is something that we observe with our senses. So in one sense faith is a spiritual sensing of God's work in our lives and in the lives of the people around us.

John Piper put it like this: "Faith is not just a responding act of the soul; it is also a grasping or perceiving or understanding act. It is a spiritual act that sees the fingerprints of God."[1]

In other words, faith allows us to perceive the unseen hand

of God at work in our lives and to celebrate as we see His finger-prints on events and circumstances that are happening every day.

Hebrews 11 shows us that when the saints of old had faith, God did supernatural things. God came through for them. People were saved from floods, lions' mouths were closed, barren parents conceived children, and infants were protected.

God is still in the business of doing that today. So why do we have such a hard time seeing it? I think it's because we persist in thinking that only what we can see with our eyes is real. But it's the other way around! What is most real, what is eternal cannot be seen with our eyes. It can only be sensed through faith.

That's why it is so amazing and empowering to our relationship with God when we begin to recognize the fingerprints of His unseen hands on our lives. Often we won't fully understand what is happening and why, but we can be assured He has only our long-term success in mind—and remember, "long term" to God is not our ninety-some years here on earth. Long term to God means beyond this life. "So we fix our eyes not on what is seen, but on what is unseen, since what is seen is temporary, but what is unseen is eternal" (2 Cor. 4:18).

The story of little Teggie illustrates how we can see the fingerprints of God. When I first heard the story of Teggie wrapped in that purple and gold Lakers blanket on the other side of the world, I had to laugh. I laughed because I knew Bruce was an avid Lakers fan. I knew that if you cut Bruce open, he probably would bleed purple and gold!

As I thought about God's kind faithfulness, I began to imagine the pure mischievous amusement our heavenly Father must have had in planting that purple and gold Lakers blanket in Ethiopia so little Teggie could be gift wrapped for his mommy and daddy.

That is the creativity of a God who knows each of us. The all-knowing heavenly Father knew years before that His children Bruce and Jaimie Watson were going to be looking at a photograph of Teggie taken on February 15, 2009. He knew what Bruce and Jaimie were going to be thinking and feeling that day. He knew the doubts that also would be on their hearts about the adoption process, the unease in their minds. *Are we really supposed to do this across-the-world adoption thing?*

I imagine that is why God marked that fuzzy purple and gold Lakers blanket for a very special mission.

As I thought about the powerful message of confirmation that blanket sent to Bruce and Jaimie when they needed it the most, I began to imagine all the things God had done to get that Lakers blanket wrapped around little Teggie. It was a mission that only God in His perfect wisdom and intimate knowledge of each of His children could design. His intimate knowledge of Bruce Watson—the same Bruce Watson who as a ten-year-old boy fell in love with the game of basketball. The same Bruce Watson who God knew would not miss a game of his favorite basketball team, the Los Angeles Lakers.

Then my imagination went one step further. I imagined the day that blanket left the textile factory in the garment district of downtown Los Angeles in 1988—perhaps on a day when Bruce Watson was eighteen years old. On that day Bruce was watching the Lakers win game 7 of the playoff series against the Detroit Pistons with a score of 108–105. On that day James Worthy and Magic Johnson became heroes to Bruce.

On that very day, I imagined, a brand-new purple and gold

Lakers blanket stenciled with a little teddy bear arrived at the hard-goods concession stand at the Great Western Forum in Englewood, California, the home court of the Los Angeles Lakers. On that day Fred Mason, a lifelong Lakers fan, bought it as a souvenir for his three-month-old baby boy, Freddy Jr., who was back home with Fred's wife in Franklin, Tennessee. Fred hurriedly paid the concession cashier twenty-two dollars and shoved the blanket into his backpack. That night he carried the backpack onto a plane, flew the red-eye back to Nashville International Airport, and drove to his little farmhouse in Franklin, Tennessee.

That was the night Fred placed the fuzzy Lakers blanket over his sleeping son. For years to come, Freddy Jr. enjoyed his favorite purple and gold teddy bear blanket. Night after cold night it kept Freddy Jr. warm in his bed or in front of a fire.

As the years went on, the purple and gold blanket began to show signs of aging. A corner was shredded when the family dog, Duke, got hold of it and envisioned it was a cat. Duke received a proper scolding, but the damage wasn't bad. Nothing a needle, thread, and a patch would not fix.

But one day Fred's wife, Isabelle, took a good look at the purple and gold blanket, which had become a bit faded and tattered. Without permission from the growing Freddy Jr. (a battle she did not want to fight), Isabelle folded up Junior's beloved blanket and placed it in a pile of donations to the Franklin, Tennessee, branch of the Salvation Army Thrift Shop. Two days later the blanket was on a truck to a donation-sorting center at Midland, Texas.

At that point an unseen hand caused that blanket to somehow land on a pile of clothing and blankets set aside to be shipped in a missionary container to somewhere around the world—a pallet to Haiti, a pallet to Honduras, a pallet to Nicaragua, a pallet to Africa. That same unseen hand guided the purple and gold blanket onto the Africa pallet that was then loaded into a shipping container and transported onto a cargo ship waiting in port in Corpus Christi, Texas.

From the Gulf of Mexico, that blanket traveled into the southern Atlantic, then around the Horn of Africa, into the Indian Ocean, and on into the Gulf of Aden, a short journey of only 13,728 miles. And when the cargo ship docked at the Port of Berbera in Somalia, the container carrying the purple and gold blanket was offloaded and driven to the warehouse of a Christian ministry dedicated to giving out assistance to needy people. On a daily basis, gifts of food, used clothing, and blankets were handed to the poorest of the poor. After spending five years and six months under a mountain of blankets in that warehouse, the fuzzy Lakers blanket finally saw daylight again. All the items that had been stacked on top of it finally had been removed, and it was ready for a new home.

The purple and gold blanket was stacked in the back of a pickup truck along with a thousand other items of food and clothing and driven to a UNICEF refugee camp. There it was handed out to a desperate young mother who did not have enough to eat. A young woman who was surrounded by daily death and starvation brought on by the sub-Saharan drought. She knew she could not find enough food to keep herself alive, let alone a child.

On that very day a tiny baby boy was placed into a container outside of an Ethiopian police station. The baby's weak cries caught the attention of a passerby, and protective hands created by God reached into the container and grasped the sickly baby, who was wrapped in the purple and gold baby blanket. Those hands were the rescuing hands of a policeman. But it was once again a powerful unseen hand that caused the police officers, for no particular reason, to drive their squad car just a little farther to the Christian orphanage, rather than to the four closer choices.

That was the day the child's photograph was taken by orphanage workers who could not even read the letters stenciled on that blanket that spelled out LAKERS in English. But it did not matter; they were not meant to read those letters. Those purple and gold letters and the message they spelled out were not meant for the rescuing officer, the orphanage workers, or the nurse who checked the little baby's heartbeat. Those English letters were meant for a family of three who would soon huddle around a computer screen, not knowing what to expect, and unsettled and undecided about what they were going to do. A family who needed a message.

That message would be carried by a purple and gold blanket, a blanket whose substantial journey had begun twenty-one years earlier. A journey that had been directed every step of the way by the unseen hand of God. A journey that had been planned long ago to send a crystal clear message to a young little family half a world away. A message that said: *This is your son. This is My plan.* A message with the telltale fingerprints of God.

This great, caring, loving, deliberate God is the reason we can have ridiculous faith. Because He is faithful to give us a message of assurance on a blanket when we need it most.

Ridiculous!

"'For I know the plans I have for you,' declares the LORD, 'plans to prosper you and not to harm you, plans to give you hope and a future'" (Jer. 29:11).

Oh God, I am so ignorant of Your designs for my life. Yet Your plans for me are more profound and more intricate than I can ever imagine. Your plans for my steps are rooted in Your deep, fatherly love that I will never fully comprehend. I am so grateful for Your loving touches on my life, the ones that are obvious and the ones I never see. Give me the faith to glimpse the fingerprints You leave behind as You prosper my life. Give me the faith to live a life worthy of Your unmatched love for me. Amen.

twelve

A FATHER'S RIDICULOUS FAITH

Promise: "I will take good care of your future."

> *"I will make you into a great nation, and I will bless you; I will make your name great, and you will be a blessing."*
> —GENESIS 12:2

Steve Powell grew up in the small town of Sterling, Indiana. He had the rare privilege of being a part of a tight-knit high school youth group from his church. There were a handful of guys and girls, about six of them in all, who were inseparable. They would hang out and have fun. They were all true friends who loved God.

One of the friends in the group was Angie Andersen. Angie was one of those people who lived a life of faith. Many times she would challenge the others in the group to jump into the adventures God had in store for them.

As the years passed, the members of the group graduated from high school. They stayed close as they set off for college and eventually went their separate ways. They did their best to keep in touch with calls, letters, and occasional visits.

In October 1997 God presented Steve with some opportunities for youth ministry, but he was burdened with fear and was reluctant to take the opportunities. One night Angie called, and they began to discuss what Steve was wrestling with.

Angie listened and then said, "Steve, let me read you something." He could hear the pages of her Bible turning.

"Ephesians 3:20–21," Angie read. "Now to him who is able to do immeasurably more than all we ask or imagine, according to his power that is at work within us, to him be the glory."

Then she said, "Steve, if God's calling you to do this, you just need to go for it. He will give you the power to do it."

Steve hung up the phone that night relieved and refreshed. He knew what he needed to do. He made that jump just as Angie had suggested.

One night about four months later, Steve received a call. Noticing the late hour, he answered the phone with apprehension.

"Hello. . . . hello."

He could tell someone was crying on the other end of the line but could not make out a word.

"Hello, who is this?"

The caller was obviously trying to get words out between hysterical sobs. Finally another voice came on the line. It was one of Steve's friends from the old high school group, and he simply said, "Steve, she's gone. Angie's dead."

"*No.* Why? How did this happen?"

Steve was told that Angie had been working at a submarine sandwich shop in Sterling. As she prepared to close the shop for the night, two men had walked in. They had not come in for a sandwich, but to rob the shop. The problem was that after pulling out guns, the men had realized Angie recognized them. Fearful she would turn them in, they had shot and killed her in cold blood.

Steve ran to his car and drove the three hours to his hometown as fast as he could. As he drove, his emotions went wild. He veered from weeping in one instant to anger in the next to sadness in the next, but all the while he was wrestling with God.

"God, how could You allow this to happen, how could You do this to Angie?" he questioned.

When Steve arrived at Angie's house, her dad embraced him and they cried together. A few days later Steve attended Angie's memorial service.

Meanwhile the police had been looking for the killers. After several days, they found the young men who had killed Angie and arrested them. Eventually they were put on trial and convicted of the murder. Through all this, Steve harbored an immense hatred toward the boys who had stolen his friend's life.

Ron, Angie's dad, saw how Steve was struggling with his feelings toward the killers. One night while they were talking on the phone, Ron said, "Steve, you know how Angie loved people?"

"Yes," Steve said, unsure of where this was going.

"Well," Ron said, "I need you to come by our house. I want to show you something."

Ron greeted Steve as he arrived at the house. He led Steve

down the hallway to Angie's room. When they entered her room, he pointed to a small, white dry-erase board hanging on the wall. Steve's eyes were drawn to the corner of the white board, where there was a list of five names. These were the names of five people Angie had been praying would come to know Christ.

As he read the names, Steve gasped. He recognized two of the five names. There in blue dry-erase ink, in Angie's handwriting, were the names of the two killers who had so brutally gunned her down.

Steve began to sob. Ron placed a gentle hand on Steve's shoulder.

"Steve, I've decided to finish what Angie started," he said. "I am going to pray for these young men. I am going to pray that God will rescue their souls."

Ron kept that commitment. Not only did he pray for his daughter's killers, eventually he visited them in prison. In time he led them to the Lord.

———

Deepening faith causes us to experience a change of values so that we desire God's promises, even over our own feelings and desires. Those promises include heaven, fellowship, and dwelling with God. Deepening faith makes us hunger to learn about the future God has prepared for us and to cherish and be satisfied by the expectation of that future.

As a result, for the Christian who is developing his or her faith, a new kind of life emerges, a life that is out of sync with what makes sense to the world. The kind of life that builds an ark in the middle of a desert—or finds a way to forgive a murder.

Ron is not a super-Christian. He is a man who has surrendered his life to the One who gives life. Ron's faith is set in the truth of what is unseen—just as Abraham's was when he was faced with the hardest decision of his life.

> Some time later God tested Abraham. He said to him, "Abraham!"
>
> "Here I am," he replied.
>
> Then God said, "Take your son, your only son, whom you love—Isaac—and go to the region of Moriah. Sacrifice him there as a burnt offering on a mountain I will show you. . . .
>
> When they reached the place God had told him about, Abraham built an altar there and arranged the wood on it. He bound his son Isaac and laid him on the altar, on top of the wood. Then he reached out his hand and took the knife to slay his son. But the angel of the LORD called out to him from heaven,
>
> "Abraham! Abraham!"
>
> "Here I am," he replied.
>
> "Do not lay a hand on the boy," he said. "Do not do anything to him. Now I know that you fear God, because you have not withheld from me your son, your only son." (Gen. 22:1–2, 6–14)

We cheer and celebrate Abraham's ultimate faith in being willing to sacrifice Isaac because we get to see the end of the story: Isaac survives. I can assure you, however, that God's request of Abraham was not met with cheers. Abraham did not answer that request to sacrifice his son by joyfully announcing, "I can't wait to do this!"

Isaac was the most precious thing in Abraham's life. He couldn't believe that this boy for whom he had waited so long was now being demanded of him. Yet despite what must have been great agony and questioning of God, Abraham eventually responded in obedience.

My question is, how could Abraham do it? How could he possibly choose to sacrifice his long-anticipated son?

The answer is *faith*.

Hebrews 11 gives us a rare inside look at Abraham's thought processes. Abraham had faith in God and knew that God had the power of life and death. He knew that Isaac could have life breathed back into him even if he died. Abraham had confidence that he would see his son again even if Isaac died.

> By faith Abraham, when God tested him, offered Isaac as a sacrifice. He who had embraced the promises was about to sacrifice his one and only son, even though God had said to him, "It is through Isaac that your offspring will be reckoned." Abraham reasoned that God could even raise the dead, and so in a manner of speaking he did receive Isaac back from death. (Heb. 11:17–19)

God had promised Abraham that he would be the father of a great nation through Isaac (Gen. 12:2). Abraham believed in that promise. He knew God's character, that his heavenly Father was trustworthy and would not lie to him or deceive him. He also knew God had power over life and death. So after what I suspect was a serious mental wrestling match, Abraham finally decided to put his faith in God and picked up that knife.

True faith in a living God changes the way you live. Sometimes it changes it from business-as-usual to *ridiculous*. But maybe not so crazy, when you're putting your faith in Someone you can trust with your hopes, your dreams, and your future.

What are you doing in your life that makes no sense? Where is the knife in your life? Is it your career, possessions, luxuries, or something you simply can't let go of? What is that thing you would never be willing to surrender to God? I challenge you to surrender it to Him and take your faith to a whole new level.

In all this you greatly rejoice, though now for a little while you may have had to suffer grief in all kinds of trials. *These have come so that the proven genuineness of your faith—of greater worth than gold, which perishes even though refined by fire*—may result in praise, glory and honor when Jesus Christ is revealed. (1 Peter 1:6–7, emphasis added)

Lord, help me discover the knife in my life. I want to have an unshakable belief in You. Give me the faith to live a life that makes no sense from an earthly perspective. Help me to live like I really believe that my faith in You is of greater value than gold. Grant me the wisdom to live a life empowered by life-changing faith in You. Amen.

thirteen

MOUNTAIN-SIZED GOD

Promise: "I will never leave or forsake you."

> Be strong and courageous. Do not be afraid or
> terrified . . . for the LORD your God goes with
> you; he will never leave you nor forsake you.
>
> —DEUTERONOMY 31:6

Daniel's story opens in approximately 605 BC, when the brutal young King Nebuchadnezzar of Babylon besieged Jerusalem and eventually conquered the city. The gold goblets and articles that had been amassed in the temple since the time of David and Solomon were "carried off to the temple of [Nebuchadnezzar's] god in Babylonia and put in the treasure house of his god" (Dan. 1:2).

These were not the only things carried off from Jerusalem. The attractive women and smartest noble children of Judah were kidnapped and taken to Babylon. King Nebuchadnezzar ordered his chief court official to "bring into the king's service some of the Israelites from the royal family and the nobility— young men without any physical defect, handsome, showing aptitude for every kind of learning, well informed, quick to understand, and qualified to serve in the king's palace. He was to teach them the language and literature of the Babylonians" (Dan. 1:3–4).

Daniel was one of these Israelites who were captured. He was probably about fifteen years old when it happened, and he would live the rest of his life in exile.

Daniel's entire world was rocked to the core when he was taken to Babylon. Everything he knew was ripped away, including his family, his home, his country. The atrocities he saw must have been horrific—likely the murder of his noble parents and the slaughter of infants dashed "against the rocks" as described in Psalm 137:9, written by a Judean musician in exile in Babylon.

Once in Babylon, Daniel was selected to take part in an elite training program for service to the king. "They were to be trained for three years, and after that they were to enter the king's service" (Dan. 1:5).

A year into Daniel's three-year training program, the king had a nightmare that completely freaked him out. After awaking from the dream, he could not sleep, so he called for all the magicians, enchanters, sorcerers, and astrologers to tell him its meaning. But the king, being the paranoid, maniacal ruler that he was, did not want to be a fool and a victim of made-up lies, which he rightly suspected this pack of wannabe "wise men" would tell him. He had not gotten to where he was by being a trusting soul.

The king devised an ingenious plan to determine if these supposed wise men were worth their salt or were just a drain on the his payroll.

The king replied to the astrologers, "This is what I have firmly decided: *If you do not tell me what my dream was and interpret it, I will have you cut into pieces and your houses turned into piles of rubble.* But if you tell me the dream and explain it, you will receive from me gifts and rewards and great honor. So tell me the dream and interpret it for me." (Dan. 2:5–6, emphasis added)

Of course, the Babylonian "wise men" complained loudly to the king that his "tell me my dream immediately or I will cut you into pieces" scheme was impossible and begged for more time. But the suspicious king would have none of it.

Then the king answered, "I am certain that you are trying to gain time, because you realize that this is what I have firmly decided: If you do not tell me the dream, there is only one penalty for you. You have conspired to tell me misleading and wicked things, hoping the situation will change. So then, tell me the dream, and I will know that you can interpret it for me."

The astrologers answered the king, "There is no one on earth who can do what the king asks! No king, however great and mighty, has ever asked such a thing of any magician or enchanter or astrologer. What the king asks is too difficult. No one can reveal it to the king except the gods, and they do not live among humans."

This made the king so angry and furious that he ordered the execution of all the wise men of Babylon. So the decree was issued to put the wise men to death, and men were sent to look for Daniel and his friends to put them to death. (Dan. 2:8–13)

You can imagine Daniel's surprise when he was awakened by Arioch, the chief of the king's guard, and led away to be executed. I'm certain he was not too happy that he and his friends were to be killed because the other "wise" idiots had infuriated the temperamental king.

Daniel asked the king's officer why the king had issued such a harsh decree. Arioch gave Daniel an explanation. Then Daniel approached the king and asked for time to try to interpret the dream. That Daniel was actually able to get time with the king when all the magicians, enchanters, and astrologers could not is a testimony to God's favor on Daniel.

Then Daniel returned to his house and explained the matter to his friends. . . . He urged them to plead for mercy from the God of heaven concerning this mystery, so that he and his friends might not be executed with the rest of the wise men of Babylon. (Dan. 2:17–18)

This was one of those crucial moments of faith. One of those desperate moments when people turn to the only One who could do anything about a helpless situation. Daniel was no stranger to this kind of life-and-death moment. During the past two years he had seen it all—the death of his family, the brutal killing of men, women, and children because they were deemed not useful. Based on his track record of faithful prayer, he undoubtedly had turned to his Creator for deliverance since the time of the fall of Jerusalem. God had come through for Daniel every time. But now, once again, he was on the brink of death. The king had decreed a death sentence, and in a few hours he would be run through if God did not intervene.

What I *love* about Daniel's response: He did not run and conspire with the wannabe wise men. He did not despair. He did not seek the "end of the world" pleasures and have one last night of carnal indulgence. No, he got on his knees and prayed and he encouraged his friends to do the same. He begged God to reveal the mystery of the king's dream. And God once again came through for Daniel and his friends. "During the night the mystery was revealed to Daniel in a vision" (v. 19).

What happened next amazes me.

Then Daniel praised the God of heaven and said:

> *"Praise be to the name of God for ever and ever;*
> *wisdom and power are his. . . .*
> *I thank and praise you, God of my ancestors:*
> *You have given me wisdom and power,*
> *you have made known to me what we asked of you,*
> *you have made known to us the dream of the king."*
> (vv. 19–23)

When I first read this passage, I felt like shouting, "Wait a minute, Daniel. How do you know you are right? Don't you want to wait until you tell the king what you've seen before you start breaking out in celebration? What if you are wrong?"

But no. Daniel had absolute faith. He was certain of what had been revealed to him. He did not need further proof. He did not need an evidentiary hearing. He did not need scientific verification. He prayed, he got direction, and he believed in what he heard. Then, without further substantiation, he broke out into praise of his Creator before reporting to Arioch that he had an answer for the king.

PRAYER INCREASES FAITH

The more I study the Bible, the more I am convinced there is a supernatural connection between prayer and internal faith. Over and over again, we see heroic acts of faith preceded by prayer. Throughout his life, when Daniel was faced with a problem, his first reaction was to pray. Even at this young stage of life Daniel knew and believed that prayer changes things.

This is a reality that permeates Scripture:

> Therefore I tell you, whatever you ask for in prayer, believe that you have received it, and it will be yours. (Mark 11:24)

And James 4 echoes that:

> You do not have, because you do not ask God. (v. 2)

I am convinced that we as Christians are falling flat on our faces when it comes to our responsibility to *ask* God. Not only does prayer develop a deep relationship with our Creator, which does amazing things for our walk with God, but it also builds our internal faith. Prayer creates trust and confidence in God. By having a regular in-depth prayer life, we begin to see the trustworthiness of our Creator, and that in turn increases our faith.

It is obvious from what we see of Daniel's life in Scripture that he knew that and lived it. Daniel was so confident in what God had revealed to him about the king's dream that he deliberately strung the king along.

> The king asked Daniel (also called Belteshazzar), "Are you able to tell me what I saw in my dream and interpret it?"
>
> Daniel replied, "No wise man, enchanter, magician or diviner can explain to the king the mystery he has asked about." (Dan. 2:26–27)

At this point the king was probably thinking, *This crackpot is just like all the other worthless liars on my payroll!* But then Daniel said this:

> There is a God in heaven who reveals mysteries. He has shown King Nebuchadnezzar what will happen in days to come. Your dream and the visions that passed through your mind as you were lying in bed are these. (v. 28)

Daniel recounted exactly the dream the king had. He described in detail an "enormous, dazzling statue, awesome in appearance," with a gold head, a silver chest and arms, bronze belly and thighs, iron legs, and iron-and-clay feet.

I can imagine the look on King Nebuchadnezzar's face as Daniel began to describe his dream in exact detail. And what happened next was nothing short of spectacular.

Then King Nebuchadnezzar fell prostrate before Daniel and paid him honor and ordered that an offering and incense be presented to him. The king said to Daniel, "Surely your God is the God of gods and the Lord of kings and a revealer of mysteries, for you were able to reveal this mystery." Then the king placed Daniel in a high position and lavished many gifts on him. He made him ruler over the entire province of Babylon and placed him in charge of all its wise men. (vv. 46–48)

It is hard to believe that this was the same guy. He "fell prostrate before Daniel." *What?* This narcissistic, maniacal king who would bow to nobody, who would annihilate cities and populations that would not capitulate to his will, who would chop people up in pieces—this proud king was actually bowing in submission before Daniel, a slave. *Ridiculous.*

MUSTARD SEED FAITH IN A MOUNTAIN-MOVING GOD

Jesus said, "Truly I tell you, if you have faith as small as a mustard seed, you can say to this mountain, 'Move from here to there,' and it will move. Nothing will be impossible for you" (Matt. 17:20).

By "mountain," Jesus meant the challenges we all face in life. And in this story, Daniel's mountain was *huge*, as big as they get. He had been sentenced to death, and his execution was imminent.

Your mountain might be that big. You or a loved one might be plagued with cancer or another terminal illness. Or your challenge might be your job, a career change, a difficult relationship, a financial or legal problem. Only you and God know what your mountain is, but God is here to help you face that mountain—just as he helped Daniel.

Daniel of all people had every excuse to be overwhelmed. Remember, he had recently lost everything from his past life, and he knew he could lose everything from his present one in a heartbeat. He could have allowed his past experience to disillusion him with this whole God thing. There was a lot of opportunity for self-pity and bitterness to sink in. You know questions had to run through his mind. *Why didn't God save Jerusalem? Why didn't God save my family? Why am I a slave?*

But Daniel didn't allow himself to give in to doubt or despair. Instead, he turned to God. The moment he remembered his God, who had kept him alive, he was on his knees begging for answers. I don't think Daniel had a two-minute prayer session before he snuggled up with his pillow and dozed off for the night. No, this was an all-nighter, a prayer marathon during which Daniel did serious business with God.

And that's what we must do too. When faced with impossible mountains, we must learn to focus on the size of our God, not the size of our mountains. We must fall on our knees and ask God for help, then get up in confidence to confront the mountains that stand in our way. Because, as Daniel discovered, we'll find that a little bit of faith makes anything possible.

Lord, when I am faced with impossible mountains in my life, help me to ignore the size of the mountains and focus on how powerful and amazing You are. Remind me when I am in the valleys of life that You will never leave me or forsake me. Do not let doubt and fear control my life. Give me strength and clarity of mind to prevent bitterness and self-pity from dwelling in my heart. Give me the tiny mustard seed of faith that can change everything. Amen.

fourteen

IT'S ONLY A SCRATCH

*Promise: "I will always be there to
help you when you need me."*

*God is our refuge and strength,
an ever-present help in trouble.
Therefore we will not fear, though the earth give way
and the mountains fall into the heart of the sea,
though its waters roar and foam
and the mountains quake with their surging.*
—PSALM 46:1–3

A few summers ago my husband and kids and I decided to rent a lake house with my sister and her family. We wanted to water ski, wakeboard, and tube. Basically we just wanted to have a fun summer vacation. After doing an online search, I found the perfect house with a private dock at Lake Nacimiento, California. I shared the listing with my sister, Shanda, and

Greg, my brother-in-love. They loved it, too, so we booked it. Everyone was excited about the trip.

I admit I held my breath when we pulled up to the address on our reservation's paperwork. Trusting pictures posted online is sometimes a gamble. But the pictures didn't lie and, if anything, this was an undersell. The house was perfect—more beautiful than the pictures had shown. We all grabbed our rooms and spent about an hour unpacking. Then we jumped in the boat to explore the lake.

Unfortunately, the next day Brice, Blake, and I woke up sick. And when I say *sick*, I mean the can't-get-out-of-bed kind of sick. Days two and three were the same—all three of us felt like we were on our deathbeds. Thank goodness for Shanda and Greg, who were able to take the girls out skiing every day while we slept.

On day four, Brice persuaded me that we needed to get some medicine. We decided to leave the lake and make the forty-five-minute drive down the hill to the nearest pharmacy.

Brice and I climbed into our SUV and headed out at ten in the morning. Normally Brice would drive, but since he had gotten the worst of the bug, he asked me to do the honors. The tree-lined road that leads to the lake is a narrow two-lane highway. As with most two-lane highways, as curves approached, the broken yellow line that allows cars to pass slower traffic changed into a double yellow line that forbade any passing.

The road ran high above the shore of the lake, and the bird's-eye view was stunning. The lake sparkled a beautiful blue as the sun's rays bounced off the water. Despite our low energy levels, with such a beautiful view we determined to make the best of the drive. Most of it was downhill as we headed to the valley below. The traffic moving our direction was quite light, but occasionally the oncoming traffic would back up behind RVs or vehicles pulling boats or trailers that were laboring up the steep mountain road.

Brice and I were deep in conversation about plans for the rest of the summer when I noticed a bit of traffic ahead in the oncoming lane. Two large SUVs were pulling boats. Suddenly, without any warning, a third car swerved out from behind the second SUV and began to pass. The driver of the small Fiat must have then seen our car coming straight for him at fifty-five miles per hour, because a split second later I saw the front of the Fiat turn quickly back into its lane. But the rapid jerk was an overcorrection. The car was traveling way too fast to respond to such a drastic turn.

Rather than tuck back into its lane, forces of gravity reacted to the panicked jerk of the wheel, and the Fiat came off the ground in a twisting flip. The little car was flipping and twisting in our lane directly in front of our windshield. Top-bottom, top-bottom, it twisted ever closer.

If this had been a movie, it would have been the greatest action scene ever. But it was real, and life and death were on the line.

I knew instantly that if the Fiat hit us at our combined speed, which was a virtual certainty, we were going to die. I felt my body go into slow motion as the opposing car rotated in midair, hurling in our direction. I could not avoid it by crossing into the opposite lane because the boat-pulling SUV was continuing forward in that lane.

Then I saw it—a bright white line on the road ahead of me. It looked fresh, as if the highway maintenance crew had just painted it. It zigzagged left, then right—an illuminated path for me to follow.

As the first SUV passed, I had enough room to slide to the left into the oncoming traffic and hopefully allow the Fiat to fly by. But it was so frighteningly close as we shifted to the left into the oncoming traffic's lane, I expected it to hit the back of our car, which would almost certainly put us into a fishtail spin.

Waiting, waiting, waiting—nothing. How did it miss us? *Impossible.* Then from the rear came a loud thud. But we were still traveling. We did not feel an impact at all. What was that noise?

I looked in front of us as the second SUV now loomed in our windshield, directly in front of us, head-on, bearing down hard. My next reaction was to nudge back into our lane to avoid it.

All of this happened in a fraction of a second. Once we realized we had avoided the second SUV, we screeched to a halt. Brice looked back and saw that the loud thud had been the Fiat hitting a large earthen berm that prevented it from flying over the cliff to the valley below.

We sat in our car, thankful to be alive. Everything was absolutely silent. I burst into tears. Brice sat in shock for a minute and then said, "Shelene, you were amazing. Like an Indy 500 driver—amazing. How did you do that?"

"There was a white line that lit up the ground," I said, "and . . . and I just followed it."

Brice and I immediately prayed and thanked God. Then we had to decide what to do next.

Since we had absolutely no cell service on the road, and knowing we could not provide immediate help, Brice suggested we continue down the road until we got cell service to call for help and an ambulance. Once service was available, Brice quickly dialed 911.

As we arrived at the bottom of the hill, we heard sirens. Several squad cars and an EMT truck passed us, heading up the hill. We would be happy to hear later that the occupants of the Fiat had survived. The soft earth of the embankment had not only prevented them from tumbling over the cliff but had cushioned the impact, saving their lives.

Meanwhile, shaken, we slowly drove to the drugstore. Brice got out of the passenger side of the car and said, "Shelene, come see this." On the back of our black Lincoln Navigator was a long white mark—not even a dent. "It's only a scratch," Brice said in astonishment. He guessed it must have been caused by a mirror or something sticking out from the body of the Fiat since we had felt no impact.

It seemed as if God was saying, "Shelene, I lit that ground up for you and held that car back. But I wanted you to know how close and how real that accident was."

Brice and I decided to leave that scratch on our car as a reminder of who is in charge of our lives. It's still there today.

———

We all place our faith in something. Driving a car requires us to place faith in people on the other side of the double yellow line. Placing our faith in things we can't see doesn't come easily for some of us. But when it comes to the things of God, we simply cannot see the essence of His power, the essence of who He is. Indeed, if we ever did see Him in His full glory, we would instantly die.

Hebrews 11:3 says, "By faith we understand that the universe was formed at God's command, so that what is seen was not made out of what was visible."

I love this passage because it reminds me that there is a real world that we cannot perceive with our senses. The physical realm, what we can see, was commanded into existence from the invisible. God spoke, and everything we can experience with our eyes, ears, tongues, noses, and skin came into existence out of the invisible. Our problem is we mistakenly go about living our lives like the invisible does not exist—until something gets our attention.

For me, the moment that I saw that Fiat flipping end-over-end in the air and headed straight for our windshield, I was certain it was the end. All the evidence in front of me convinced me that my death was at hand. But God's unseen hand had a different plan.

Was it an angel that lit that path? Was it God illuminating my mind to show what moves needed to be made? I don't know the answer. I just know that for a split second, by God's providence, His invisible world was actually somehow visible to me. Our mission here on earth was not yet done. God was not finished with us yet.

Lord, our lives are so fragile. Thank You for the reminder that it is by Your providence that we take our next breath. When I am faced with trouble, prompt me to remember You are with me to help me navigate the storm. Please constantly remind me that what I can experience with my senses is not all that is going on. Help me to live my life with the unseen spiritual realm constantly in mind. Help me to always remember that true safety is only found in You. Amen.

part four

PUTTING FAITH INTO ACTION

After we have established a foundation of faith by knowing God and engaging His promises, then we need to act. The fastest way out of a spiritual rut is to do something courageous for God—something out of our normal comfort zones, something that forces us to rely on God in faith. Nothing has exploded my faith more than seeing God work out impossible situations.

And yes, that first step into the unknown can be petrifying. I definitely know what it's like to be frozen in fear and doubt and worry before I take the leap. But I've learned to keep telling myself, *God has this!*

Because He does.

fifteen

CAN YOU SPELL THAT?

*What more shall I say? I do not have time to tell
about Gideon, Barak, Samson and Jephthah,
about David and Samuel and the prophets, who
through faith conquered kingdoms, administered
justice, and gained what was promised.*
—HEBREWS 11:32–33

Dave and his wife, Lynn, were on a car ride home from a fun
Fourth of July weekend when they finally made the life-changing
decision they had been wrestling with. They would step out in
faith and do something radical. Together they would do something to help the needy here in America. On that car ride, Dave
and Lynn came up with the name of a charity, Children's Hunger
Fund (CHF), which they would start out of their garage.

Dave was a graduate of Westmont College in Santa Barbara,
California. He had always planned on going into international
banking. His grandfather had served as treasurer of the Billy

Graham Crusades and had been instrumental in the founding of World Vision International. His father had been the executive vice president of World Opportunities, International, for forty-one years after serving in Korea to launch World Vision's orphan programs. But Dave had always figured he'd be the one in the family making money to fund charity—not the one actually running a Christian ministry.

In hindsight, it seems only natural that Dave would join in the family legacy. But when he was young, he didn't see it that way. In fact, even after he had left his job and founded CHF, he struggled with knowing he was where God wanted him.

Something had happened many years earlier that eventually influenced Dave's decision to go into ministry. After graduating from college, Dave had visited the cancer ward of a children's hospital in Honduras called the Love and Life Center. He'd been taken into the terminal ward to see the children determined to be beyond hope. The boys and girls, about sixty of them, were crowded into a small, three-room facility. Tattered beds lined the walls, and the sounds of children in pain filled the air.

Dave's heart had been broken. He had never seen such suffering, such hopelessness and despair. He'd thought he'd found his life's work—to care for these few children, to ease their pain, and to provide them a little bit of hope before they died. He'd been convinced he was going to move to Honduras to become an advocate for the facility. But somehow that hadn't happened. It turned out that God had a different plan.

Dave and Lynn were only six weeks into launching CHF when Dave received an unexpected phone call. It was Joe Mayes, the director of the Love and Life center in Honduras, where Dave had been so impacted a few years earlier.

"This may seem like a strange request," Joe explained, "but I feel like I am supposed to ask you if you can get us a cancer drug that is made in the United States. We have seven children in the center who are suffering from cancer and are going to die without treatment."

Dave's first thought was *I don't know anything about cancer drugs or where to get them.* But then he thought of the time he had spent in the Love and Life clinic, and young faces flashed across his mind.

"Well," he said hesitantly, "we have never had a medicine donation before, and I have no idea how to go about getting one, but I am happy to try. I just don't want you to get your hopes up."

"I understand," Joe said.

"Tell me the name of the drug and I will see if there is anything I can do."

"Sure. It's cyclophosphamide."[1]

"Can you spell that?"

"It's spelled C-Y-C-L-O-P-H-O-S-P-H-A-M-I-D-E," Joe said, slowly enunciating each letter.

Dave had never heard of the drug, but he jotted down the name on a pad next to the telephone.

Before they got off the phone, Dave suggested they pray for the seven children. They prayed together, begging God to comfort these kids and, if it was His will, to somehow provide this medicine.

After the prayer, goodbyes were exchanged and Dave hung up the phone. Just as he hung up the handset, before he could even take his hand off the receiver, the phone rang. Thinking it was Joe again, instead of his normal greeting of "CHF," he simply said, "Hi."

It was not Joe.

"Hello, I am calling for Dave Phillips," the voice asked in a formal tone. "Is he available?"

Flustered at himself for not answering the phone properly, Dave answered, "Yes, this is Dave Phillips."

"Oh, hello, Dave. You don't know me, but I was given your name by someone who thought you might be able to help. I work for a pharmaceutical company. We'd like to make a donation of cancer treatment medication. Do you have a need for anything like that?"

Dave just about fell out of his chair.

"Well, well . . . we might. Let me just ask, what is the name of the medication you were wanting to donate?" Dave said as calmly as possible.

"Sure. It's called cyclophosphamide—that's spelled C-Y-C-L-O-P-H-O-S-P-H-A-M-I-D-E. We have forty-eight thousand vials we'd be willing to donate if you could find a need for it."

Dave looked down at the notepad next to the telephone and stared in disbelief at the letters he had jotted down moments earlier: C-Y-C-L-O-P-H-O-S-P-H-A-M-I-D-E. A chill went through his body.

"You are not going to believe this, but I literally just got off the phone with the director of a clinic in Honduras who was asking for that exact medication," Dave explained.

An excited telephone discussion followed, and by the time Dave had hung up the phone, CHF had secured a donation valued at eight million dollars' worth of the medication. The company even offered to airlift the medicine to Honduras and anywhere else in the world that had a need for the medication. After Dave got home that night and shared with Lynn what had just happened, all she could say was, "Wow, wow, wow!"

Within two days the lifesaving drug had been flown to the treatment center in Honduras and to twenty other locations.

It was only at that point that Dave and Lynn were completely convinced they had made the right choice to scratch their own plans and step out in faith to start CHF. God was confirming they were doing exactly what they should be doing. Over the years since then, tens of thousands of children and families have been cared for and shown love by CHF's work with the poor.

It was a little more than ten years later that I would meet Dave Philips on a plane. We both were traveling to Uganda and happened to be seated right next to each other. Without that meeting, our charity, Skip1.org, would not have been founded.

It is only when we step out in faith, willing to walk away from our own plans, that God can put us on an adventure like no other. That is when God will show us His unseen hands— His hands that can move time and move resources wherever and whenever He wants to.

Dave and Lynn are not some super-Christians; they are just regular people willing to trust God. They were willing to take a step of faith into what they felt God was leading them to do.

Sometimes a step is all God requires—a willing heart undivided. God just gave them a little wink to confirm they were on the right track.

Oxford Dictionaries defines a *miracle* as "a surprising and welcome event that is not explicable by natural or scientific laws and is therefore considered to be the work of a divine agency."[2]

Yes, God can and does work miracles to bring help here on earth. Sometimes He intervenes in how nature works and makes it work differently—supernaturally. If you doubt this, you need look no further than Hebrews 11:29–35, which gives multiple examples of God interrupting the way nature normally works—the parting of the Red Sea (v. 29), the crumbling of the great walls of Jericho (v. 30), the sealing of the mouths of lions when Daniel was in their den (v. 33), the ability of Shadrach, Meshach, and Abednego to walk unscathed amid the raging fire (v. 34), and the resurrection of a child who had died prematurely (v. 35).

For God, the laws of physics are not really laws at all—to Him they are optional. Sometimes when we trust Him in faith, God chooses to suspend the rules and acts to move mountains. That's what Dave experienced with that phone call. If you try to calculate the odds of that happening, your calculator will freeze up. It was clearly God's plan that at that particular time, that particular drug was supposed to drop into Dave's lap.

Only God sees the whole picture. But what a privilege when we get to be just a tiny part of it. How sad it would have been if Dave and Lynn had not stepped out in faith and had completely missed it.

Lord, I want to have courageous faith. I want to have faith so that I can see Your fingerprints surrounding my life. I pray that You give me the strength to live in such a way that this world is not worthy of me, but that I might be worthy of the glory You have prepared for me. Amen.

sixteen

THE MASTER BEDROOM

A few years ago at Thanksgiving we decided to join our friends Francis and Lisa Chan and their family in San Francisco. The Chans had moved from pastoring our church in an affluent Southern California community and eventually ended up doing inner-city ministry in an area of San Francisco called the Tenderloin. This area happens to be one of the most dangerous areas in all of San Francisco.

On Thanksgiving morning our two families met at the rescue mission in the "loin," then broke up into groups. Each group was assigned to a building that looked like a hotel. Despite the grand outside appearances, we learned that the buildings, which one hundred years ago had been the finest hotels in the city, were now something totally different. The city kept the facades of the existing structures looking like hotels, including the 1930s-era signs: The Hamptons, The Four Seasons, and The Ritz-Carlton. But when you got inside, you quickly realized these were no longer hotels. Each of these structures had been converted into government-subsidized low-income housing.

Each of the older Chan kids had picked a "hotel" to love and serve in. They had personal knowledge of who was behind every door and what their stories and situations were. It was amazing. We split up and followed the Chan kids to their respective sponsored hotels. We carried boxes of hot Thanksgiving turkey dinners, one for each resident. We met all kinds of people. Families with incredible stories dined and broke bread together. We had an unforgettable Thanksgiving.

Back at the rescue mission, Francis introduced me to the head chef who had prepared all the food for the thousands of people who had been fed that day. His name was Shawn Gordon. (And yes, this was the same Shawn Gordon, whom I spoke about earlier, who would later direct Project Bayview.) I thanked Shawn for his hard service. When you are not Jesus, feeding thousands of people at the same time is not easy.

"So, Shawn, how was it that you came to work at the mission?" I asked.

"Well, that's a long story," he said.

"I have time."

"After I got out of prison for the second time—"

"Wait—you were in prison?"

Shawn explained that he had spent twelve years in some of the most dangerous and violent prisons in America. Before I could stop myself, the Diane Sawyer in me came out. "Why did you go to prison?" I was hoping he was not going to say murder.

"I was raised in a house that was full of violence," he answered. "It had all the ingredients for the perfect disaster. My father was stabbed to death. He was stabbed twenty-eight times, the last one hitting him in his heart. He died in my front yard in the arms of my grandfather. A short time later, my grandfather was also stabbed to death on the streets of San

Francisco. My mother, who had been raised in the foster care system, was broken and hurt; and her life was out of control. She made decisions that were detrimental to my sister and me. I felt like carry-on luggage."

"As if my life wasn't messed up enough at that time, one day my mom told me she had AIDS," Shawn continued. "Back then all we knew about AIDS was you were going to die. The moment she told me that, I knew I had to cry out to someone. I had never cried out to anybody, certainly not God."

Later I learned that Shawn's mom had died of AIDS.

"What was that like?" I asked.

"Take a pit bull that's been chained up in the backyard. When people walk by they throw rocks at him. They kick him; he hasn't been fed in days. When my mother died, it was like that pit bull was let off his leash. If the people who were supposed to nurture me, love me, and protect me—if they were the ones who were hurting me and destroying me every day— what do you think my thoughts were about the people outside this house? I assumed they wanted to kill me. And I used this assumption as justification for what I did on the streets. My friends thought I was crazy because I was willing to do stuff that most people in the hood aren't willing to do. I ran these streets doing everything I could do."

The next time I visited San Francisco, I got to spend time with Shawn, and he told me more of his story.

At twenty-four years old, Shawn went to prison. There he continued the addictions he had learned on the streets. He consumed alcohol and took psych meds, plus a number of other drugs they were able to get in prison. He also made plans.

"I did push-ups and I plotted," he told me. "I meditated

on what I was going to do to this community upon my release. That's all I did for five years—plot. There was one thing in prison that other inmates won't do, and that's violence toward the guards, the COs. That's a lose-lose situation. But I kept choosing to lose and so I spent a year in the shoe. The shoe is like a prison inside of a prison. They say you are so off the hook that you can't even be with other inmates, so they isolate you. They would slide my food under a little slot just like you see on TV. I spent a year in there, and all I kept doing was more and more push-ups."

Shawn pulled out a picture of himself in the solitary confinement of the shoe. I could not believe my eyes. His chest, shoulders, and arms looked like he was a non-green version of the Incredible Hulk.

"Oh my gosh, Shawn, I guess you did just do push-ups," I said.

"I was like a lion trapped in a cage, pacing back and forth for 365 days a year. I was that lion. And after five years they released me back to the community. Can you believe that? I told you what I had been plotting. I was going to get back everything they took from me. I didn't last twenty minutes on the streets and I was already back into my addiction."

After that first stint in prison, Shawn was out for less than a year and a half. During that time he met a beautiful woman—beautiful inside and out. Carolyn was different from Shawn. She came from a different world.

"I didn't know what love was. I didn't know what it was like to be a husband or a father. Everything that was modeled to me was built off destruction. But I fell in love with Carolyn, we got married, and we had a beautiful baby girl. We got a house with a little picket fence. I fell in love with our little girl. I call her my miracle baby. It was the first time anything had started piercing my callous heart. On the surface I was trying to play house with my little family, but my actions brought me right back to prison."

Carolyn was nine months pregnant with their second child and his daughter had just turned one when Shawn was sent back to prison. "I was sitting back in this prison cell. I was broken, thinking, how did I get here again?"

While in prison this time Shawn met a man he thought was crazy. This man kept coming back to Shawn's cell. Shawn would tell him to "get out of here" in a not-so-nice way, but he just kept coming back.

"I thought he was crazy because he was doing thirteen years and he looked happy. He had something that I didn't understand at the time. He had peace. Peace was very foreign to me."

The man had something he wanted to give Shawn. It was a Bible. And as Shawn began to read that Bible, something happened. "I was someone who had stopped crying before I was a teenager, but now tears were falling down my face. What was going to happen to my life? My kids? My wife? That was nine years ago when that guy handed me that Bible, and I haven't put it down since."

Shawn had been sentenced to do seven-and-a-half years. He ended up doing six.

"I did everything I could to turn my life around while I was in prison. I went back to school and got my GED. I went to college, then seminary. I took advantage of everything the prison system had to offer, and I consumed books upon books upon books."

During the ten years Shawn had been in prison, he wasn't one of these guys who just got in line. He was a shot caller. He was the guy who made decisions about other people's lives. Inside prison there was a microuniverse inside of a universe. "We had our own money, currency, food. Even the guards were on our payroll."

Then God began to convict Shawn's heart about being in a prison gang.

"In prison the gangs with the larger numbers win. The crazier you are, the safer you are. But now I was changed, and I was trying to use my position as a voice of reason. The problem was, I was trying to serve two masters at once. I was still trying to hold on to my gang position, but I was also trying to do the right stuff. Basically, I was contaminating all the good stuff I was doing. So with ten years in, I decided I was going to get out of the gang. Coming from being a killer whale in prison to becoming a baby minnow was the scariest thing I had ever done. But it was the best thing I ever did."

When Shawn was released from prison, he was dropped off at the place where all his troubles began: right back in the Tenderloin—"the devil's playground," as Shawn calls it. His wife and children lived two hours away.

"Look at me—no one was hiring me." I looked at the tattoos that ran up his neck and the teardrop tattoo coming out of his eye and agreed that the San Francisco bankers were probably not clambering to hire him. He did not have a résumé because the items that would appear on it would almost certainly land him back in prison.

Shawn tried covering up his tattoos with makeup. He went on job interview after job interview. Denied, denied, denied.

He started to feel lost again—that familiar feeling he had experienced so many times as a boy.

Then one day Shawn happened to be walking down the street when he "saw a Chinese guy who I recognized." In prison, Shawn had read a book called *Crazy Love.* It was a book that changed his life. The Chinese guy was Francis Chan, the author of *Crazy Love.*[1] "I was so excited and nervous as I went up to meet him. I was just stammering. When I left him at the sidewalk, I was embarrassed. I must have looked like a stammering idiot."

A few weeks later Shawn ran into Francis again at the rescue mission where he had picked up work as a cook. "We got to know each other. He heard my story and how I was struggling with my new life."

After hearing about Shawn's life, Francis said, "Shawn, you are my brother. You have nowhere to live? No place to go? Move in with me."

Shawn could not believe this invitation. Was this guy for real?

"I'm not kidding. Move in with me and my family."

Within a few weeks Shawn had moved his wife and kids into the Chans' house. He later realized that Francis and Lisa had moved out of their master bedroom and into their son's little room so Shawn and his family could have a little more room and some privacy.

"This man was modeling what it looked like to be a husband, a father, a friend. Who does that? Me, my wife, my children—we all got to live there and got to live out this thing called 'church.' So when I moved in with him it was not like we opened up the Bible and went over Scriptures all day long.

We just did life together. One man took the time to invest into another man—me."

I was blown away by Shawn's story and by the act of sacrifice Francis and Lisa had done for this man. Our son, Blake, was also blown away by Shawn's story. He first met Shawn that Thanksgiving weekend we spent in San Francisco as a family. He was so affected by Shawn's story that Blake invited him to speak at his high school for an event in front of a thousand students. You could hear a pin drop in the auditorium. All the students were on the edges of their seats. After telling his story, Shawn began to describe the massive change faith had made in his life.

"Today let me tell you what I'm not. I am not that lost, broken little child anymore. I know my value, my worth. I am a husband, a father, a pastor. My kids are being nurtured. I am now going back into those hoods. I am dedicated to going back into those places to be the hands and feet of Jesus, to reach out to people the way I wish someone had reached out to me. I work in a part of San Francisco called Bayview-Hunters Point. There you are six times more likely to be killed than any other place in San Francisco. I run a discipleship program called Project Bayview."

As I sat there listening to this ex-felon speaking to this group of college-bound students, many of whom were headed to the most impressive college institutions in the country, I could not help but smile.

This is what faith does, I thought, *It replaces a hardened broken heart with a new one. It gives hope to a truly hopeless situation. It puts an ex-con who went to the school of hard knocks on a stage, mesmerizing a bunch of Ivy-League-bound students. That is awesomely ridiculous.*

But through it all, I could not help but think that Shawn Gordon's story is not just the story of one man with ridiculous faith, but two. Shawn's story would not be the amazing tale of redemption and salvation that it is without the faith of another man. A man who was willing to stand next to a person our society had rightfully rejected because of his actions. A man— and his wife—willing to give up the most sacred place in their home, the master bedroom, all to live out faith.

It was that action of ridiculous faith that spoke more to Shawn than a thousand sermons ever could have.

It was an act of faith that refused to be bound by fear.

It was an act of faith that rejected convenience and took immediate action.

It was a testimony of what God can do and what God wants to do through us.

That is the kind of ridiculous faith we are called to live out.

Lord, give me the guidance and discernment to know when I need to act in faith. Help me to place my fears and my desire for comfort and convenience into Your hands. Grow in me a heart of compassion for the lost, lonely, and hurting. But most of all, Lord, give me the strength to put my faith into action. Amen.

seventeen

#SENIORS SKIP

*So we fix our eyes not on what is seen, but on
what is unseen, since what is seen is temporary,
but what is unseen is eternal.*
—2 CORINTHIANS 4:18

As with many high schools across the country, homecoming
at Oaks Christian School is a big deal. A really big deal. So
when it came time for the senior class at Oaks Christian to
plan their last homecoming float, they wanted to do something
spectacular. By long-entrenched tradition, the homecoming
floats are the pride of each year's senior class. Past floats at
homecoming have been some of the most extravagant ever. I'm
not kidding.

Several years ago a senior class managed to acquire a
Hollywood set of a pirate ship that was being discarded. (This
ship was from the set of a famous series of pirate movies. The
name won't be mentioned here for legal reasons, but you would

recognize it instantly.) They purchased the pirate ship set and stored it in a warehouse for a few years, knowing they would use it for their senior year finale. When their senior year homecoming came around, they hauled it from storage and mounted it on the flatbed trailer of an eighteen-wheel semitruck. The class rigged the ship with sails in the school colors, then added cannons that shot fireworks, a band of singing pirates, and a high-wire duel between Peter Pan and Captain Hook.

Another senior class built a giant ship named after *The Love Boat*, complete with singing and dancing sharks and beachgoers. You get the idea. Senior-year homecoming floats are a big deal at Oaks Christian. Of course, as a matter of class pride, every year the seniors refuse to be outdone by their lower classes. So there is constant pressure for "bigger and better." The price tag for a senior float could run as high as ten thousand dollars.

Not this year, though. This year homecoming was going to be different.

During the past few years I had been the guest speaker at several Oaks Christian School chapels. Because of those chapels, the students were familiar with our charity, Skip1. I had spoken to the students about forgoing some luxuries and helping the helpless instead. Our Skip1 slogan, "Skip Something. Feed a Child," was well known to the student body. Sometimes the students would even joke about skipping things they did not want to do.

"Did you finish your homework?"

"Naw . . . let's skip it and feed a child." (Laughter)

"Did you bring your uniform?"

"Nope. Skipped it." (More laughter)

After a particularly challenging brainstorming session about what the seniors were going to do with this year's homecoming float, Blake's classmate Ryan Hiepler made an offhand joke to Riley Phillips. "Hey, why don't we just skip the float?"

They laughed and gave each other high fives. Then Riley stopped.

"Ryan, you know what? That's actually a great idea. We could skip the float and donate what we would spend on it to feed hungry children."

"Actually, that does sound like a great idea. Let's call Blake."

Soon my son Blake was on the phone. Ryan and Riley were pitching their idea about skipping the float. Blake loved it.

"But guys, we need to get the entire class on board, and that is not going to be too easy. Everybody wants to win; it's a matter of class pride."

A few days later Ryan, Riley, and Blake had a meeting with the powers that be at the school—the deans and the headmaster—and then they met with the senior class leadership team. Blake explained to the team that the year before he had loved being in charge of constructing the amazing two-story Atlantis float. For the three minutes it took to drive in front of the home crowd of alumni, students, and spectators, he had been thrilled. But the next morning had found him in the parking lot with his dad and one other student, using a power saw to cut the giant wooden superstructure of Atlantis into two-foot-long pieces, all to be hauled away in the back of the family SUV as winter firewood.

"That was an empty feeling," he explained to his classmates. "It seemed like such a waste of money, time, and energy."

Ryan, Riley, and Blake shared their vision of the senior class doing something different this year. They wanted to do something that would last, something that would leave a legacy.

"What if we skipped the float and instead built a food kitchen overseas through Skip1.org?" Blake asked. "That way kids could have lunch every day."

The students' response was humbling. They were all on board. They absolutely loved the idea. Many realized "skipping" the float meant they would not win the float competition, but they agreed the sacrifice for something bigger was worth it.

The seniors decided to keep their float idea a secret. The entire class would have to keep it under wraps. They set up special team meetings in homes, away from school. The team spent the next few weeks deciding how they wanted the reveal to happen on homecoming night.

———

The long-awaited night of the homecoming game finally arrived. The stands were packed with several thousand people. The seniors had kept their secret well. Their float was hidden behind a giant maroon curtain that had been attached to pipes surrounding the flat bed of the semitruck. None of the other classes had been able to see what was behind the giant curtain and the anticipation was killing everyone. This year's homecoming theme was the seasons: winter, spring, summer, and fall. The freshman fall float drove by, decked out as a Starbucks, complete with beautiful autumn leaves falling. The sophomore spring float had flowers and trampolines. The junior winter float was all decked out as a snow globe.

The senior float rolled down the track until it reached the middle of the stands and then came to a halt. As the curtain began to move, the homecoming fans moved to the edge of their seats, straining to see what was behind the curtain. Finally it swooshed back to reveal—*nothing*! The bed of the truck was completely empty! Then Ryan Hiepler and class president Grace Zilli appeared, surrounded by hundreds of their classmates holding up large posters of children's faces whose lives were going to be changed by the kitchen the class wanted to build.

Ryan explained to the crowd that all money usually invested in float building would go toward establishing a kitchen ministry in northern India. He said that skipping the float and leaving a legacy was something the entire senior class felt they'd never regret. "We all can skip one thing once in our lifetime for the sake of someone else!" he told the crowd.

Seventeen-year-old Ryan had already donated a thousand dollars of his own money to help build the kitchen. The students asked everyone at the homecoming game to skip something in their lives and help raise the money needed to build the kitchen. As spectators left the game that night, they walked the red carpet, dropping their loose change in receptacles the students held out or even adding checks or cash. Ten thousand and five hundred dollars later, the kids had done it!

I was thrilled as I sat in the stands that night. But I had no idea about the emotional journey the night was going to take me on.

As days, weeks, and months passed, the seniors' skip float was all but a cool memory. Then one afternoon in January, Blake called me from school. "Mom, is there any way I can meet with you and Dad for lunch? I want to talk with you about something."

I called Brice, and we met Blake for lunch at Hookburger.

"Remember the float we skipped?" Blake asked.

"Of course."

"I don't know if you remember, but our school is taking a team of students to north India, where Skip1 is building that kitchen. Well, the trip has been booked for nearly a year, but I have just been offered a spot to join the team traveling to the boys' home where our kitchen was built!"

"Wow, Blake, that sounds amazing!" I said on the outside. But immediately fear began to rise up inside me.

Blake continued. "A kid had to drop out, so Dr. Lisea asked if I could join the team. I would like to use my own money and go on the trip."

"Well. When do they leave?"

"Next month. They kind of need an answer right away so that I can turn in my passport and get a visa. Right away. As in *today*."

Before I could look at Brice, he said, "Blake, of course you can go. I think this could be a real life-changing trip for you, especially being able to meet the children in India and to see firsthand the effect skipping the float made on their lives."

"That was what I was thinking," Blake answered.

I was feeling a little out of the loop. These two basically had Blake's bags packed already. I chimed in. "Well, who else is going? What adult teachers are going? Do you need shots to travel to north India?"

"Mom, it sounds like you need to read your own book [*Love, Skip, Jump*]. You are kind of freaking out."

"No, I'm not," I said defensively. "I'm just getting the facts."

"The facts are that Blake is eighteen years old, and he will be traveling with the King of the Universe. I think this is a divine appointment," Brice said. "It's not every day you and your friends have an idea to skip a homecoming float, get an entire senior class to agree, raise more than ten thousand dollars, and in the same year, before heading off to college, get to see the kitchen and meet the kids you did it all for."

"True," Blake agreed.

"I wish I could join you, son," Brice said. "You are going to have a blast."

Really? God . . . What's the deal with me? I feel like I take two steps forward in my faith, then three steps back. Do I really think Blake is safer with me than with You, God?

That night on a walk with Brice I shared my concerns. After listening to my whining about the dangers of northern India, Brice calmly said, "Honey, why don't you play out your biggest fears about the whole trip with God, then ask yourself if God is still God?"

That night when I went to bed, I had it out with God, imagining every disease, kidnapping, car crash, plane vanishing, torture, and death scenario. I felt God was telling me, *Shelene, through all your fears, I am still on the throne. Trust Me.*

As the trip grew closer, God kept bringing me to Scripture regarding the ridiculous actions people took in following Jesus—cutting a hole in someone's ceiling for their friend, climbing a sycamore tree to see Jesus, believing if they could just touch His cloak they would be healed, stepping out of that boat and walking on water. These were all acts of ridiculous faith. As the trip grew closer, I had a supernatural peace that Blake was with the ultimate traveling companion—his Creator.

———

In February Brice dropped Blake off at the Los Angeles International Airport for his flight to Dubai and then on to New Delhi—twenty hours in all. It was a few stressful days before we heard from Blake. But we finally received a text with some pictures saying, "I'm in India!"

I was thrilled when my phone chirped with a FaceTime call from Blake. In an excited but travel-weary voice, he explained that they were leaving in the morning to travel up to northern India and that I would not be hearing from him for the next several days because there was very little Internet service at the boys' home where they were going to stay.

Okay, Lord, he's in Your hands.

The next four days were nerve-racking. We knew the political climate in northern India was hostile, with tensions between the various religious factions across the world reaching a boiling point. The Muslim and Hindu populations in the area where the students were staying seemed to harbor a deep hatred toward Christians. I had to stop watching the news because the daily news stories from the troubled areas confirmed my fear was warranted. But there were daily blogs with photos from the teacher chaperones who were able to get a Wi-Fi connection long enough to upload a few pictures and a description of the day's activities.

On the evening of the fourth day, my phone chirped with a FaceTime call from India. My heart stopped for an instant.

It was Blake. They had left northern India and were now back in New Delhi.

"Mom, we actually suffered some persecution," Blake said with excitement. He went on to explain that when they were up north the local authorities had received an anonymous tip that Americans were proselytizing the local citizens, a crime punishable by imprisonment according to local laws. The students were rushed to the head pastor's house for several hours while the local investigators were assured the American students were only there helping with projects at the boys' home.

Blake was absolutely thrilled to experience that temporary persecution. "Mom, it's like what the Bible says, 'everyone who wants to live a godly life in Christ Jesus will be persecuted'" (2 Tim. 3:12).

"Well, son, I am proud of you, and I am so glad you are okay and back to safety."

"Don't worry, Mom. We are going to be fine."

We spent a few more precious minutes talking. Then he had to sign off.

I hung up the phone relieved. Well, relieved in one sense. I had seen my son's face and I knew he was safe. But I also had felt a strange, ominous feeling of unease.

That night I went to bed late. I had become so restless that when Brice said, "Honey, let's go to bed," my reply was, "Honey, I'm going to stay up and watch some TV. I just know I won't sleep right now."

I channel surfed for the next hour, laughed at a crazy game Jimmy Fallon had cooked up for some unsuspecting celeb, and discovered that I needed some sort of facial lift, at least if the infomercial were to be believed. Finally, when the remote dropped out of my hand after a momentary lapse into sleep, I surrendered it to the coffee table and went to bed. The instant my head hit that pillow, I drifted into a deep, solid sleep.

I was awakened by the familiar FaceTime chirp. I jolted up in bed, fumbled for my phone, and simultaneously glanced at the clock: 3:07 a.m. At first I was relieved to see it was a call from Blake's phone. But as I pushed the FaceTime accept button, the image that appeared on the screen was not Blake. It was one of the teacher chaperones on the trip, Susan Issac. The image on the phone was so dark I could barely make her out; it was as if she was calling in the dark.

"Hello?"

"Shelene, it's Susan Issac," she said in a tone barely above a whisper. "I wanted to let you know right away—we have a situation here."

"What do you mean 'a situation'?"

"About an hour ago the power to our hotel was cut off. We were told to stay in our rooms and we did, until we heard some loud banging. I made my way to Dr. Lisea's room and—"

"Susan, stop. Are you guys okay?"

"Everyone here is okay. But Shelene, some men have taken Dr. Lisea and Blake."

"*Taken?* What do you mean *taken?*"

"They were marched off by some masked men who have seized control of the hotel."

What? No. Oh no! Lord, help them! Then I asked, "What are you doing?"

"We are staying right here. The Indian counterterrorism authorities are with us."

"What can I do?"

"See if you can get some help from that end—a Navy SEAL team or something."

There was a loud banging sound. "I've got to go," she said in a whisper.

"Susan, what was that sound? Susan—"

The screen want black. I sat there in a panic. My mind began to race, thinking of people I knew with political or military connections. *We need to inform them right away so they can do something.*

Then suddenly my phone rang again, and I answered. Someone said, "Shelene, Shelene, Shelene."

Someone kept calling my name over the phone. It was so annoying.

"Stop calling my name!" I said. "Stop bothering me."

"Shelene, Shelene. Wake up, Shelene—"

My eyes flew open. I sat up straight and gasped for air. Brice was right there, staring me in the face. He was gently shaking me.

"Honey, honey, you're okay. You've been dreaming."

"It's Blake," I said in a panic. "He's been kidnapped! I got a call at 3:07—"

"No, honey, you have been having a nightmare. Blake is just fine. Remember, we just FaceTimed him a few hours ago. The team is in New Delhi, safe and sound."

I rubbed the sleepy sand from my eyes. "A dream? It was just a dream?"

I grabbed my phone and searched my call log. No FaceTime call at 3:07 a.m. The last call was from Blake at 9:34 p.m.

A flood of relief washed over me. I sat on the edge of the bed, tears of relief streaming down my face. "I thought he was gone. I'm so sorry."

Brice put his arms around me and held me. "Don't be sorry. Everyone's okay. Don't be sorry."

It took me about fifteen minutes to compose myself. When I could finally look at Brice, we started to laugh.

"You woke me up, saying I had to call the president right away."

"Well, hey, if you can get him on the phone, go ahead. I have a trip I would like to take him on that would benefit a whole lot of children."

———

My whole life, fear had ruled me. Now those old fears were still coming out, even in my dreams. But with God's help, I determined to do my life differently. I was going to surrender it all to the Lord. My control. My kids. My very life. I was going to live by faith.

When Blake got back from India, I could see what the trip had done for him. His whole perspective was changed. His eyes were focused not on the temporary but on the eternal. "So we fix our eyes not on what is seen, but on what is unseen, since what is seen is temporary, but what is unseen is eternal" (2 Cor. 4:18).

The class of 2015 had their eyes fixed on the right thing. Yes, they sacrificed first place in the float competition, but what was unseen on that flatbed that night was eternal. They will never regret the sacrifice of skipping a float to leave a legacy that will last a lifetime. And neither will I.

Lord, help me to have the faith to realize that it is the unseen things that are eternal. Help me to live a life that proves my life is not about the earthly things I can see, but about heavenly things, things that really matter. Help me hold on loosely to things that are meaningless and that will be gone tomorrow. Amen.

eighteen

TEXAS HOLD 'EM

Do not forget to show hospitality to strangers,
for by so doing some people have shown
hospitality to angels without knowing it.
—HEBREWS 13:2

It was a one-on-one game of backyard basketball on a
beautiful Malibu, California, kind of day. Jeff was only in
fifth grade but was quite an athlete. His dad, Adam, was much
stronger and more skillful but was enjoying the intensity his
young competitive son brought to the game. Adam would give
Jeff some game without completely slamming his son.

As the game got going, Jeff started getting frustrated
because things weren't going his way. He took the basketball
and threw it as hard as he could at the pole holding up the
basketball hoop. The ball hit the pole, bounced back, and hit
Jeff right in the solar plexus, knocking the wind out of him.
The kid had an arm on him, that's for sure.

Adam walked over to pick up the ball, letting Jeff feel the consequences of his lack of self-control. *Maybe you'll learn from this, Son,* he thought. But just as the thought crossed Adam's mind, he turned to see Jeff go limp and fall unconscious, slamming face-first into the court. Adam ran to his son and found him out cold on the court. "Wake up, Jeff," he urged, as he held his son's cheek in his hand. The twenty seconds that passed seemed like an hour, but Jeff finally started moving and came to.

A minute later Jeff was able to sit up. His face was imprinted with the waffle pattern of the plastic squares that lined their backyard sports court.

"Are you okay, buddy?"

"I think I'm okay, Dad. What happened?"

"You knocked the wind out of yourself, then you fell and hit your head. Hard."

"Oh, okay," Jeff said. Adam got Jeff up and handed him some water.

A few minutes later Jeff repeated the earlier questions.

"I think I'm okay, Dad. What happened?"

"Uhhh, like I said, Jeff, you hit your head," said Adam, growing concerned over the odd repeat of the question. "We are going to get you checked out."

He helped Jeff into the car and headed over to the urgent care facility in Malibu, which was not far away. Then he called his wife, Trisha, who was with their daughter at a Brownie outing. On her way to meet her husband and son, Trisha called her sister-in-law and asked her to start praying.

When Trisha arrived at the clinic, the staff took her to join Adam and Jeff in the exam room. As soon as Trisha entered the room, Jeff got a huge smile on his face, and stretched out his arms and shouted, "Mommy!"

Trisha leaned in for a hug and could see the waffle cuts on his face.

Jeff turned to his dad and asked, "What's wrong with my finger? What happened?"

"We were playing basketball, Son, and you fell and hurt your finger."

"Oh, okay," Jeff said.

About a minute later, Jeff looked at Trisha as if she had just arrived, got a huge smile on his face, stretched out his arms, and called out, "Mommy!"

Once again Trisha leaned in for a hug.

"What's wrong with my finger? What happened?"

"You were playing basketball, Jeff, and fell and hurt your finger."

"Oh, okay," Jeff said.

The third time they went through the same set of questions and answers, Trisha looked at Adam. "Are you kidding me?"

Adam smiled hesitantly and said, "He's been doing this since he came to."

The cycle kept repeating like a scene from *Groundhog Day* or *50 First Dates*, until finally the medical staff arrived.

"Folks, we can't treat your son here."

Adam was alarmed. "Why not?"

"He needs an MRI and possibly other testing that we are not set up for here."

"Where should we go?"

"We have called for an ambulance to transport him right away to Saint Paul's Hospital in Santa Monica."

———

Trisha rode with Jeff in the ambulance and Adam followed in his car. As they pulled away from the urgent care clinic, Jeff started throwing up. The paramedics began discussing where to take Jeff. They decided he needed to be taken to UCLA.

"What does that mean? Why are you switching hospitals?" Trisha asked nervously.

One of the paramedics said calmly, "Well, Santa Monica is where we go for minor head injuries. Your son's symptoms have changed and indicate clear head trauma, so we are taking him to UCLA."

By now Trisha was very concerned.

They pulled into one of the ambulance bays at the UCLA emergency compound. Jeff was quickly admitted and put in a room with sheets for walls.

"Mom, I have to go," Jeff told Trisha.

"What? You have to go? Go where?"

"I have to go to my play-off game."

"Jeff, honey, you don't have a play-off game."

"What do you mean?"

"Play-offs are over."

"Well, did we win?"

"No."

"*No?*" Jeff burst out in tears. "We lost?" Tears continued streaming down his face.

Two minutes later Jeff repeated the same dialogue again. The sixth time it happened, Trisha couldn't take it anymore and had to walk out of the room for a minute. She was thinking, *They are probably going to come back and tell me that he has a concussion, that we need to watch him over the next twenty-four hours, and then send us on our way.*

Instead, when the doctor came in, he said, "We think it's possible your son has bleeding on the brain. We need him to stay and have another MRI in about two hours."

Trisha was beside herself. The only person she knew who had experience with concussions was a family friend, a former pro football player for the Pittsburg Steelers.

"I've got to call Mark," she told Adam.

She dialed Mark's number and told him what was going on.

"The doctors say Jeff has a moderate concussion," she said, and then described the strange repetitive behavior. "What do you think?"

"I don't know, Trisha," he said. "Mine have always been mild; I've never had a moderate. It sounds pretty serious."

"Shoot! I thought moderate was a good thing."

After the phone call, she put on a brave face and went back into the room.

"Hi, Mom, I'm really hungry. Can we get something to eat?"

"No, Jeff, you can't eat right now. They are going to do another MRI. Why don't you try and get some rest?"

"Well, do you have any cards so we can play some Texas Hold 'Em?"

"I don't have any cards."

Jeff turned over for about fifteen seconds, then turned back around. "Mommy, I'm hungry. Can we get something to eat?"

"No, Son, you can't eat right now. Remember, you are having an MRI soon."

"Well, do you have any cards so we can play some Texas Hold 'Em?"

Jeff repeated the same routine over and over again.

Trisha needed to get some air and some water. She needed to do *something* and maybe find some cards as they waited for the next MRI.

She walked out of Jeff's room. As she did, she noticed a college-age young man sitting on the ground, playing with a new deck of cards.

"Hello," Trisha said. "Where did you get that deck of cards?"

"These? I brought them from home. My roommate cut his hand, and I figured I'd be here awhile, so I brought them."

"Oh, okay," Trisha said and left to search for the gift shop to buy a bottle of water and maybe a deck of cards. Unfortunately, the gift store was closed. The young man was still sitting on the floor when she returned. He stopped her and said, "Hey, what is your son here for?"

"He has a concussion and they are not sure if he has bleeding on the brain."

"Oh," he said, "please take my cards."

"Are you sure?" Trisha said. And then, not wanting to be rude, she said, "No, that's okay. I am not going to take your cards. Thank you anyway, though."

"No, I insist. Please take them. I am going to be out of here soon anyway."

"Well, okay."

The young man looked Trisha in the eyes as he handed her the deck of cards. "I will pray for you."

Trisha smiled. "That really means a lot. Thank you."

"Trisha, your son is going to be okay," he said with confidence. "Just be sure you two play some Texas Hold 'Em."

Strangely, Trisha felt an instant peace. With a nod she turned and walked back into Jeff's room.

Texas Hold 'Em, she thought. *How the heck did that kid know? There is no way that kid heard the conversation Jeff and I had. And how did he know my name?*

Before she could freak out, the nurse entered the room again and asked Jeff if he knew where he was.

Jeff looked up at her and said, "UCLA?"

"Great. Look at that!" the nurse said. "You're getting better already."

"Actually, it wasn't too hard. I just read your badge," Jeff said, pointing to the nurse's UCLA name tag. In that instant, Trisha knew that Jeff was going to be all right.

————

As Trisha turned to ponder all that just happened with the student in the hall, the cards, and the strange Texas Hold 'Em comment, she peeked through the glass window on Jeff's door and recognized Dr. Steve Erickson, a parent from Jeff's school. Dr. Erickson was in charge of the ER. Trisha tapped on the locked door window, and the doctor turned around.

"Trisha," he said, "what are you doing here?"

"Jeff fell and hit his—"

Before she could finish, he blurted out, "Oh, you're the head injury! I was supposed to leave more than an hour ago, but it's been extra crazy here today."

As Dr. Steve looked over Jeff's chart, Trisha told him they

were waiting for another MRI. They were worried Jeff might have bleeding on the brain.

"No," Dr. Steve said, "I am not going to let Jeff have another scan. I would never let my own child have another one. He then offered to send Jeff's scan results to the top doctors at their homes.

"What I need you and Adam to do is to take Jeff home and let him rest. No TV, reading, or other activities. Basically he can watch the paint peel on the ceiling. I will be in touch tomorrow, as soon as I get feedback from the doctors about his scans."

"Thank you," Trisha and Adam said.

As she sat down, a thought ran through Trisha's mind. *This is amazing.*

Trisha quickly ran out to the hall to where the young man had been sitting, so she could thank him for the prayers. But he was gone.

Trisha began thinking about the guy in the hall. From the moment he had told Trisha that Jeff was going to be all right and that he would be praying for her, everything had changed. Who was that guy?

The Bible tells us we might entertain angels without knowing it. "Do not forget to show hospitality to strangers, for by so doing some people have shown hospitality to angels without knowing it" (Heb. 13:2).

I used to brush off stories like Jeff's as luck or coincidence. When I heard them, in the back of my mind, I would think to myself, *Oh that's just wishful thinking.* But after I spent some time in the book of Hebrews, it became clear to me that God in His faithfulness and goodness sometimes lets the unseen world mix with our physical world. Hebrews 13:2 tells us that

1) people have entertained angels in the past without knowing it, and 2) we could have such an encounter—thus the need to warn us to be hospitable. Any one of us could be entertaining angels.

The Bible refers to angels at least 294 times (depending on the translation). They are a constant presence throughout the Old and New Testaments. And the Bible says one of their major assignments is to minister to those who are believers. Hebrews 1:14 says, "Are not all angels ministering spirits sent to serve those who will inherit salvation?" And for those who have "made the Lord their refuge" (Ps. 91:9) the Bible says that "he will command his angels concerning you to guard you in all your ways" (v. 11). But how and when God will command His angels to intervene with natural forces is and will remain a mystery.

Was the young man in the hospital hall Trisha's angel sent by God? She will never know for sure until the day she stands before her Creator and asks Him. But whether he was an angel or just someone God allowed to minister to Trisha in that moment, God was showing His faithfulness to her, Adam, and Jeff. A faithfulness worthy of great faith.

Jeff made a full recovery and went on to become a high school basketball star. He now attends the University of Southern California and still loves to play the game.

Lord, help me to practice hospitality to everyone who crosses my path. Should You in Your wisdom choose to intervene with the natural or decide to send an angel my way, help me to be faithful to the reason You are intervening in my life. Let my wonder about Your angels inspire me to live faithfully in Your ways. Amen.

part five

LEAVING A LEGACY OF FAITH

We are each living out a life story and leaving a legacy. It will either be a legacy of faith or a legacy of something that will be meaningless in the future. Every one of the heroes of faith mentioned in Hebrews 11 had a life story worth telling because faith could be seen in their actions. It was tiny, mustard-seed faith all grown up. And it did indeed move mountains.

What will your life story be? Ask God to start a faith movement inside you that will sustain you on your quest to know Him, follow Him, and live out what He has in mind for you—so that generations to come can look at your life and be strengthened for their own faith journey.

nineteen

FIRST-CLASS SEATS

All these people were still living by faith when they died. They did not receive the things promised; they only saw them and welcomed them from a distance, admitting that they were foreigners and strangers on earth.

—HEBREWS 11:13

Our entire team of fifteen people had boarded the plane. We were sitting on the runway in Lima, Peru, headed home to Los Angeles. We had just finished an amazing five days of caring for the poor and needy. We had met with local church leaders and prayed with their congregations. We were just about to say good-bye to a wonderful, friendly country.

As I settled into my seat for the evening flight, I took out the book I had brought and began to read. Just then the flight attendant's voice came over the PA system, delivering a message in Spanish. I was able to pick out a few words, but for the most part I was lost. I was about to unbuckle my seatbelt and find our interpreter, who was six rows or so behind me, when the flight attendant started into an English version of the announcement.

"Ladies and gentlemen, our flight is overbooked. We need four passengers to get off this flight, and we will give you a two-hundred-dollar travel voucher and tickets on tomorrow night's flight to Los Angeles. If you are interested, please push the call button and we will come to you."

Silence. No takers.

Another five minutes went by and the flight attendant started walking up and down the aisles of the plane, looking passengers in the eye and imploring them to accept the new offer. "Is anyone willing to help us and get off the plane? We need three people to get off [apparently one poor dupe had taken the first offer]. We will give you four hundred dollars and tickets on this same flight tomorrow night to Los Angeles."

Brice looked over at me with a look that implied, "What do you think?" I shook my head, indicating I was not in the mood.

The silence among the passengers was heavy as the attendant continued to plead her case. As for my group, we were all exhausted after a long week of visiting the slums, playing with the children, and meeting with families. I was even more ready for this plane to get off the ground and in the air because I had a middle seat in coach and knew it was going to be a very long flight. At least Brice and my Pops, Al Dickens, sandwiched me in, so I could lean against them when I got tired.

After another ten minutes, realizing that until a few people got off this plane, it was going nowhere fast, I had an idea.

"Brice, would you get off if we got double what they are offering plus first class tomorrow?"

"I'd seriously consider it. Do you know how many kids we could feed with twenty-four hundred dollars?" he said. "But honey, they are not going to double the offer."

"We'll see," I said, with a twinkle in my eye.

"Excuse me," I said to the flight attendant. She turned around and made her way to my seat.

"Yes?"

"Here's how I can help you. The three of us [pointing to myself, Brice, and Pops] will get off this plane for eight hundred dollars each, American cash, no travel vouchers accepted. We also would need seats in the first-class cabin on the next flight to LAX tomorrow night. We would need the airline to provide us hotel accommodations. And, of course, we would need transportation to the hotel."

She smiled and said, "Just one moment please."

Pops looked at me as if to say, *Were you going to ask us about this?*

Oops. But Pops, who never minds making money, seemed to warm up fairly quickly to the idea of making eight hundred dollars, and since he is six feet, three inches tall, the extra legroom in first class would be a welcome change from coach.

"They are never going to agree to this," Brice quietly said to me, "but if for some reason they are that desperate, I will happily get off this plane."

A few minutes later the stewardess came back. "I want to inform you that LAN Airlines has agreed to your terms, only we need to send you a check for the twenty-four hundred dollars. If you are agreeable, please get your things, and I will have an agent take you to the flight desk and process your paperwork."

"That will be acceptable," I said. "And thank you—that money will be put to good use feeding a lot of hungry kids."

After walking back through the first-class cabin as we exited the plane, Brice got a grin on his face. He had seen the beds in that section.

Now, before you think I'm a genius, and decide you want to fly all over the world with me, hold everything. You see, in all the deal-making excitement, I forgot to consider one *huge* factor. It did not really hit me until we were off the plane and were trying to communicate with the woman at the flight desk. *No habla español.*

This was different from our Peru experience so far. You see, for the entire week we'd had our favorite interpreter, José Luis, with us. He had been our guide, interpreter, friend, comedian—you get the idea. When we needed to understand anything, José was always there. It was like second nature to have José interpret—*all the time.* It felt so natural to rely on José that we had not realized what it would be like without him. Unfortunately for us, José was still sitting on the plane, and by this time he was at thirty thousand feet, speeding home to Los Angeles.

Basically, other than *hola* and *adios,* I speak no Spanish. Neither do Brice and Pops. So we had some difficulty making the necessary arrangements.

LAN Airlines was nice enough to find an employee who could speak at least broken English to finish our vouchers for the hotel, meals, and cab, and to finalize everything for our check. The airline worker took us outside the terminal to a long line, where we waited for the next cab.

I expected a nice, clean, yellow cab like I was used to in

the United States. When our "cab" finally pulled up, I thought I was on a *Punked in Peru* episode. The cab looked as if it had been in a demolition derby. It may once have been a silver 1972ish Toyota Corolla, but the car had so many dents that had been hammered out and painted over with gray primer, the only original paint still visible was the roof and a few patches on the hood and trunk. Every corner of the vehicle was crumpled like an accordion, and both the taillights were broken, with little or no red lens. The rear bumper was held on by yellow rope tied to the frame of the car, but the rope had loosened and the bumper was sagging.

I started to object, but Brice said, "Let's just take it and get to the hotel. It's one in the morning, and the next cab probably won't be much better."

"Okay, you're probably right," I agreed.

The driver ran to the back of the car and unwound a piece of wire that apparently served as the lock for the trunk. When he finished unwinding it, the trunk popped open but was only secured by one hinge. The cabbie ran over to the sidewalk, grabbed our luggage, and piled it into the trunk. Of course, there was no chance our three large suitcases were going to fit into the tiny trunk, but no matter. He just lengthened the wire and secured the trunk lid in a half-open position.

As we piled into the cab, the LAN interpreter told the driver to take us to the Double Dolphin resort hotel. At least that's what we thought when the interpreter kept repeating, "Double Dolphin, Double Dolphin" and the cabbie kept nodding vigorously.

Just as we pulled away from the curb, it started to rain. Soon we were in a heavy South American downpour. Never in my life had I seen such a storm. Worse yet, the driver did not turn on the windshield wipers. The windshield was so flooded with water that nothing but the dim flashing lights from oncoming cars could be made out.

Brice tried to communicate to the driver to turn on his windshield wipers but did not know the right words. He kept saying "wipers, wipers" to no avail. Finally he resorted to holding his hands in the air and waggling his index fingers in synchronized motions as if they were tiny wipers. That did the trick. The cabbie nodded his head vigorously and reached down to flip a switch. The wipers came on, and we instantly understood why he had not turned them on in the first place.

Screech, screech, screech. The driver's-side wiper had no rubber whatsoever. The metal arm with its spindle fingers designed to hold the rubber blade was now etching across the glass.

"Stop! Stop!" Brice shouted. There was no reaction. Finally Brice yelled, "Hey!" to get the driver's attention and simultaneously signaled to cut the wipers by drawing his right hand across his neck and shaking his head in a "kill it" signal. Whether this was taken as a threat of what Brice would do to the cabbie if the screeching didn't stop or simply as an instruction to cut the power to the wipers, I was not sure, but it got the message across rather quickly.

As the rain came down harder and harder, the driver rolled down his window and with his jacket wrapped around his hand, he tried to clean off the water and grime from the windshield—all while still driving at fifty miles per hour!

We are all going to die! flashed through my mind several times, and at this point I was thinking the middle seat in coach looked pretty good compared to this. The twenty-four-hundred-dollar check that was going to be sent and the first-class plane tickets in my purse meant nothing at the moment.

Looking at Pops and Brice, I mouthed the words, "I'm sorry." Then I started to pray.

"Lord, please don't let us die. Lord, please get us to the hotel safely. Lord, please don't let this man kidnap us for ransom money. Lord, please don't let us get in a car accident because no one can see out of the windshield. Please, Lord. Please, please."

It's amazing how our minds work in times of stress. I had a full-length horror film running through my mind. All I needed was the popcorn and the Diet Coke.

Just when I was ready to scream and demand that the driver pull over so we could walk the rest of the way, he made a sharp right turn and we squealed to a halt in the valet parking area of the hotel. I jumped out of the car as fast as I could and ran up to the front desk.

"Do you speak English?"

"Yes, ma'am."

"Great. Can you please get us our room keys ASAP? Our rooms should be all set up by LAN Airlines."

"Yes, ma'am, I have them right here."

"Great! And does the hotel have a shuttle to the airport?"

"Yes," she said.

"Can you please book the three of us on the shuttle for our flight back to America tomorrow night?"

"My pleasure." The lady smiled.

"No, the pleasure is all mine, *really*."

With that we made our way up to our rooms. I hit the bed and didn't wake up until eleven thirty the next morning. The shuttle back to the airport was wonderful, mainly because the driver spoke English.

My first-class seat is still and will mostly likely forever be the best seat—well, bed—I've ever had on a plane.

I have often thought about how lost and helpless we felt that night in a strange city where everyone we came in contact with could not understand us. We felt like the foreigners we were, and it did not feel good.

Have you ever felt like a stranger in a foreign land when thinking about your life? When you are interacting with your world, do you ever feel like your values are so different from everything you see around you that you are basically in exile from your homeland?

I am not talking about being divisive. To the contrary, I am talking about being radically different by showing God's love. I am talking about a motivation for life that is different from our culture's motivation—a way of living that is selfless, not selfish. Have you ever felt like such thinking is foreign to everyone around you?

If you have, you're not alone. Hebrews 11 gives a long list of God's people who had that experience: "All these people were still living by faith when they died. They did not receive the things promised; they only saw them and welcomed them from a distance, admitting that they were foreigners and strangers on earth" (Heb. 11:13).

God promised to make Abraham the father of a great nation, but Abraham did not see it in this life. God promised

Sarah, Isaac, and Jacob a land for their people, a city to call their own. They did not see it in this life. What the saints of old came to understand was that as God's children they would always be strangers in this world.

I have come to understand, too, that I am a stranger in this land.

The life of faith at its core is a life that looks forward to an amazing post-death future. While some of God's promises are for this life—*peace* that transcends all understanding (Phil. 4:7) and *joy* in the face of trials (James 1:2–3)—most of God's promises are about a spectacular future once we finish with life on earth. The future for a Christian is a magnificent opportunity, one that includes the promise of heaven (better than the best mansion you can imagine) and the promise of dwelling in harmony and relationship with God Himself.

And because of that looking-toward-the-future attitude, Christians who begin to understand that their real home is not on this earth suddenly experience a change in priorities. Our values begin to change.

Fancy cars, luxurious houses, the finest clothes, and the latest cool electronics were once the desire and obsession of my life. But after I got a *glimpse* of the promise of an indescribable heaven and a small taste of the richness of a relationship with my Creator, my values completely changed. Things that had once seemed so impressive and worthy of my pursuit have grown strangely dim and unimportant.

Hebrews 11:13–16 explains that the heroes of the faith recognized that they were just passing through here. They understood they were really just strangers and foreigners on this earth—that *real* life was going to be later.

Dear friends, I urge you, as foreigners and exiles, to abstain from sinful desires, which wage war against your soul. Live such good lives among the pagans that, though they accuse you of doing wrong, they may see your good deeds and glorify God on the day he visits us. (1 Peter 2:11–12)

God, help me to have a future-looking perspective on my life. Help that to penetrate the way I live. Help me to be a stranger in this world by living a life that is selfless and not selfish. Help me to illustrate Your love with my actions. Amen.

twenty

LIFE STORY

Instead, they were longing for a better country—a heavenly one. Therefore God is not ashamed to be called their God, for he has prepared a city for them.

—HEBREWS 11:16

I had met Orville Hiepler a few times at school basketball games or other events, where he was watching his highly talented grandchildren dominate on the courts, fields, or in just about anything they tried. Even from the beginning, when I did not really know him, I had always been impressed with him. I wondered how it was even possible that the oldest living person I knew—ninety-three at the time—had more energy than just about anyone else in the room. He always had a warm greeting and an amazing smile, and always remembered something about my life. "How did Brooke's game go? Did you guys finish that kitchen in Rwanda you were building?

What is happening with Brice?" It was astonishing. He remembered things I had even forgotten about myself.

As time went on, I learned more about Orville. He started life as a prairie farm boy from Springbrook, North Dakota. He grew up in the Roaring Twenties, lived through the Dust Bowl and the Great Depression, and had shown up at college two weeks late because he was helping his father on the farm. The better I got to know Orville, in fact, the more he impressed me. Then we were invited to a birthday party and I learned what kind of man Orville Hiepler really was.

Our remarkable friend Mark, Orville's son, happened to be born on Christmas Day. So after a full day of celebrating Christmas, we gathered that night to celebrate Mark. We were moving from the family room to gather around the dinner table when I noticed Orville had carried a bulging manila file folder into the dining room. He set it aside while dinner was served. But after dinner, before dessert, Orville called for everyone's attention.

"I have a few words I'd like to share," he said. We all fell silent out of respect. Orville pulled out the overflowing manila folder and placed it on the table. When he opened the folder, I saw it contained a stack of yellowed newspaper articles.

Orville proceeded to pull four newspaper articles out of the folder and began to summarize each one. There was an article in which a high school basketball coach talked about Mark's character, an article in which Mark was interviewed as the president of his college, one that named him as one of the top forty most influential attorneys under the age of thirty, and yet another one that placed him among the top hundred most influential lawyers in America. Orville proudly read a sentence or two from each article.

The chosen articles, even though they were separated by forty years and had different authors, all had a recognizable consistent theme: Mark serving others on and off the basketball court, and in and out of the courtroom, where his life purpose is to be a crusader for a noble cause, not just another case handler. After proudly reading the glowing reviews of his son's amateur and professional accomplishments, Orville said, "I am here tonight to testify that those things said about my son are true and I want to wish him a wonderful birthday."

When he finished his speech, Orville replaced the articles in the manila folder, which contained every newspaper article about Mark that had ever been published—from the time Mark was a little boy, right up to the present.

I left dinner that night in awe of a godly man whose job as a father, even at ninety-three, was not done. He was still pouring his life into his son.

Orville is special not just because he is in his midnineties but because he is in his midnineties and still cares. He cares about people. He cares about the growth of his church. He cares about his grandchildren's high school. He doesn't just attend church or grandparents' day at school (which at his age would be impressive enough), he advocates constantly with a loud voice and vivid hand expressions for how things could be better, how we could reach more souls for Christ, how we could do more good things together. And he continually draws attention to the good things others were doing.

A few years after Mark's party, Orville's ninety-fifth

birthday was approaching. His kids wanted to throw him a special birthday party in recognition of that milestone.

"What kind of party would you like?" Mark asked. "We could take a party bus to a Lakers game. Or we could invite all your friends and have a celebration at home."

"Son, at my age I don't want to party," Orville said. "I want to preach."

"Well, then, preach you will, Dad. Preach you will."

———

On Sunday, February 8, 2015, we pulled into the parking lot of Good Shepherd Lutheran Church in Camarillo, California. This was the church where Orville had been a pastor for twenty of his seventy years in ministry. The marquee sign outside of the church read, "Preaching this Sunday at 8:30, Dr. Orville Hiepler—Celebrating 95 years of God's faithfulness."

Those driving by might have assumed that the ninety-five-year celebration was for the church itself. Little did they know it was a birthday celebration for the man who would occupy the pulpit that Sunday morning. But we knew it, and we could not wait to hear Orville do the best possible thing on his birthday.

Orville took the stage wearing a black suit and black shirt with a minister's white collar. An American flag was pinned to his lapel. Introducing Orville, the pastor of the church pointed out that when Orville was born, the Civil War had only been over for fifty-six years.

A warm round of applause greeted Orville when he took the pulpit. People had traveled from across the country to celebrate this day—people whose lives had been touched by this man's faith. His wife of seventy years, who suffered from dementia, was in the audience.

He spoke from the heart, his voice at times booming and at other times dropping to barely above a whisper. "This is a high point in my ninety-five years of life. At my age I may use my notes a little more; I may talk faster because I'm limited to a certain number of minutes. It reminds me of the lady, a senior citizen, who was speeding down the freeway. The police officer stopped her. 'Lady, why are you going so fast?' She said, 'At my age if I don't hurry, I will forget where I am going.' Forgive me if at my age I'm in a hurry. I don't want to forget what I am going to say!"

Orville went on to speak with the pure wisdom that only a long and well-lived life can bring. In reflecting on his life, he boiled it all down: "Without Christ, life is a dream without substance. It's progress without a purpose. It's a journey without a goal."

As he was closing, Orville spoke about all he had to look forward to, the "beautiful chapters of my life yet to be written." This was a man of great faith, and true to form, even at ninety-five he was still looking forward to what would come next.

Orville Hiepler's is surely a life story that makes God smile.

We are each living out a life story. Every one of the heroes of faith in Hebrews had a life story worth telling because faith was seen in their actions. Everything we think, say, and do each day tells a story about who we are and what we are about. It's a story that's written every day, every week, month, and year by every choice we make, each desire we act upon. And either that story will be pleasing to God or God will be ashamed of what we did with our lives. Nothing pleases God more than for us to have a life story characterized by faith.

Hebrews 11:16 illustrates how an entire list of heroes, despite their flaws, lived lives focused on the unseen. They desired the eternal things of God rather than the temporary things of this world. "They were longing for a better country—a heavenly one. Therefore God is not ashamed to be called their God, for he has prepared a city for them."

I want God to be unashamed of me and the life story I am living. I want God to be proud that I call myself a Christian. But most of all, I want to put a smile on my Creator's face by living a life that is focused on the unseen, a life of great faith. How can we do it? How can we live lives of great faith, lives longing for things not of this world? The answer is found in Romans 12:1: "Therefore, I urge you, brothers and sisters, in view of God's mercy, to offer your bodies as a living sacrifice, holy and pleasing to God—this is your true and proper worship."

It's about giving ourselves as a living sacrifice. No matter where we are in our relationship with God, offering up ourselves to our Creator for His purposes must be the highest and most important calling of our lives—from the first day we give our lives to Christ until the very last breath we take. It is a greater opportunity than anything that school, marriage, career, family, or service can offer us.

The importance and significance of this opportunity is often forgotten and lost as our lives become routine. Sometimes it is seen as a duty rather than the amazing prospect that it is.

Before I can hope to put a smile on God's face, I have to offer myself as a living sacrifice to Him. Orville knew that. As a result his life story is an amazing example of a life well lived in faith.

I am learning that as well, and I pray that I might be able to live a life story whose chapters are filled with astonishing adventures created, authorized, and led by our amazing God.

Adventures of ridiculous faith.

Lord, may my life story leave Your fingerprints on the people I encounter in my life. I offer myself as a living sacrifice for You and Your service. I want to live my life unashamed, with You by my side every step of the way. I want to know You, and I want You to know me—every fiber of my soul. Amen.

twenty-one

MARVELOUS

*Therefore, since we are surrounded by such
a great cloud of witnesses, let us throw off
everything that hinders and the sin that so easily
entangles. And let us run with perseverance
the race marked out for us, fixing our eyes on
Jesus, the pioneer and perfecter of faith. For
the joy set before him he endured the cross,
scorning its shame, and sat down at the right
hand of the throne of God.*

—HEBREWS 12:1–2

The first time I met Katherine Dickens, she was the
epitome of good health. Brice and I had arrived at her husband's property management office for a meeting to sign an
office lease for my talent agency. We were a bit intimidated as
we ascended the glass and black marble spiral staircase to the
all-glass conference room for our meeting with Al Dickens.

As we sat in the reception area, we heard a deep, resonating sound clacking its way up the spiral staircase, accompanied by what sounded like panting. Brice threw me a curious look, as if to say, "What the heck is that?" Within a few seconds, a massive black-and-white Old English sheepdog appeared at the top of the stairs. The dog went straight to Brice, and Brice went straight for the dog. Brice knelt down on one knee and gave that fluffy, lovable animal a big hug and rubdown.

Just as the two of them were getting acquainted, a classy-looking woman in her forties reached the top of the stairs.

"Nikki!" she called.

Immediately the dog (apparently Nikki) left Brice and heeled at his mistress's side.

"So sorry about that. He has not seen me in a couple of weeks and got a bit excited."

"Oh, no problem," Brice said. "I love your dog. When I was a kid, I worked at a pet store and saved all summer for a dog that looked just like him."

"Really?" the woman said warmly. "I'm Kay." She extended a hand. "Nice to meet you. We just got back from a trip to Aspen, and I came to pick him up."

Kay looked as if she had just stepped out of the pages of *Fitness* magazine. We later learned that she ran two or three miles every other day and exercised other ways in between. She was beautiful, talented, and I would also learn later, a woman after God's own heart.

Kay smiled at the receptionist and looked Brice and me in the eyes with a big smile and a nod. "It was so nice to meet you." With that she bounded down the stairs with Nikki by her side.

Little did I know that was the last time I would see her like this.

———

Theirs had been a true love story. They had married later in life, very appropriately on February 14, Valentine's Day. Al adored her. She truly was the love of his life. He would call her sweetheart and she would call him sweet pal.

Al was accustomed to being able to fix things. He was a self-made man, an entrepreneur. In addition to his property management company, which handled his substantial holdings in commercial real estate, Al owned a very successful construction company.

He was an architect and a general contractor. He was great with money, and his partners were happy to have him running things. You could say, as far as world standards go, that Al and Kay Dickens had made it. They had the money and means to live a very comfortable life in beautiful homes across the country, to drive nice cars, and to travel the world.

On August 15, 1993, Al and Kay went out to a nice dinner. When they got back to the house, she sat on their bed with her head in her hands.

If only I could get rid of this darn headache, she thought.

"Sweet pal, could you get me a wet washcloth? I'm not feeling well," she asked.

Al left her side and went to the sink to wet a washcloth. Seconds later, while he was still at the sink, she blacked out.

Unable to revive her, Al rushed to the phone and dialed 911. By the time paramedics arrived, Kay had regained consciousness and was coherent. As a precaution, the paramedics took Kay to the hospital. Al grabbed his jacket and followed the ambulance in his car to West Hills Hospital in West Hills, California.

After doing some preliminary testing, the doctor explained, "Mr. Dickens, your wife has an aneurism in her brain. We need to do emergency surgery and put in a metal clip to contain it, or she will die."

Al told the doctor he would like to get a second opinion from UCLA or Cedars.

"If you take your wife, you will need to sign her out against medical advice. Your wife's aneurism is like a grenade, and the pin has been pulled. If you move her, you take the risk of killing her."

Al reluctantly agreed to the surgery. He didn't want to lose his wife. The next day, Kay was taken in to surgery to treat the aneurism. During the procedure, Kay suffered two devastating back-to-back strokes.

In the weeks that followed, the effects of the strokes became fully known. Kay was completely paralyzed. Her hands and arms had curled up against her body. She couldn't walk, talk, or even feed herself. Because she could not chew or swallow, a gastric tube was placed down her throat into her stomach to give her liquid food so she could survive. The brain damage from the strokes had also changed her outgoing bubbly personality.

True to his nature, Al determined to do everything in his power to fix this new problem. When the doctor finally agreed to let him take Kay home from the hospital, he turned their elegant house into a physical and mental rehab center.

Because it was three stories, with a long flight of stairs

leading to the master bedroom, the living room and dining room now became Kay's makeshift rehab bedroom. The fancy furniture was removed. The gorgeous fourteen-person dining table was replaced by the best hospital bed money could buy. The elegantly crafted sofa and chairs were replaced by a multitude of rehabilitation apparatuses: a standing machine (since she could not stand), a large ranging table (where the physical therapist could work her out), various cables and weights to help with stretching, and a hot-water spa tub.

Before Kay's sickness, she and Al had just finished building their dream retirement house overlooking the ocean in Montecito. The house had so many stairs and split levels that it was totally unsuitable for a wheelchair. So Al went to work designing and later building a new house that contained an entire hospital wing for Kay. This house even featured an elevator and private accommodations for the full-time nurses who would stay the night with Kay.

I detail how I came to know Al in my book *Love, Skip, Jump*, so I will not retell that story here. Suffice it to say that taking a moment out of my life to stop and pray for Al while Kay was first in the hospital fused a bond for a lifetime. Al became "Pops" to me and I was beyond blessed to watch the love story between Pops and Kay lived out for the next twenty years. It was not the kind of love story told in Hollywood movies. It was much harder, heartwrenching at times. But Pops was going to live out the vows he made to his wife to love, honor, and cherish her in sickness and in health till death did them part. I had the privilege of hiring the caregivers who would take care of Kay during the next twenty years. Caregivers like Marian, who in time would become family.

As time went on Kay began to gain limited use of her right hand. Her progress was very slow, but eventually she was able to feed herself, and the brightness I had seen in her eyes the very first day I met her gradually returned. With time new neural pathways were made in her brain and she began to speak, though usually in a very faint voice, barely above a whisper. But every once in a while, when she was excited, she would take a deep breath and her voice would boom as if she were yelling out a cheer. She startled us a few times.

Kay would never be able to walk again but she could carry on a conversation, and her shining eyes and brilliant smile warmed everybody's heart.

Most remarkably, in Kay I had the opportunity to see what a true woman of faith looked like. Kay had a joy and contentment that was not of this world. She was confined to a wheelchair, and dependent on her caregivers to move her, clean her, and feed her. Yet every time I would ask her how she was doing, she would give me the same reply. "Marvelous, Shelene. I am doing marvelous." She would say it with the most beautiful smile that just lit up the room. Those looking at Kay in her wheelchair without the use of her arms or legs might be tempted to object, but one look at her smile and we were all convinced she really was "marvelous."

Kay never complained about anything. Given her circumstances, nobody would have blamed her if she had yelled, screamed, or even just said, "This is frustrating! I wish I could walk or brush my own teeth." Kay's circumstances could have created bitterness and even understandable rage, but her faith wouldn't allow it.

The biggest thing I believe Pops and I learned during those

twenty years was that Kay was healthier than most of us when it came to her heart. Kay knew her Creator. Early on in her life she had surrendered her heart to her Lord and Savior Jesus Christ. She loved Jesus and would get up at four thirty almost every morning to spend time with Him.

Pops had always respected his wife and her devoted love to God and to him although he hadn't shared her faith. Before getting sick, Kay would often invite him to church on Sunday. Whether Pops joined her or not, she had rarely missed a service. But she had never been bitter toward Pops for not going. Before and after her stroke, Kay had an unwavering faith. A ridiculous faith in an absurdly, unbelievably good God.

After the stroke, Pops realized with the love of his life sick, his money couldn't buy her health back. One day Pops and I were at lunch, and I will never forget what he said. "I'd give away every dime I have to have Kay healthy again. I can always make more money."

Pops also realized that, even with her brain damage from the strokes, Kay still wanted to go to church. I bet you can guess who took her every Sunday after that. Pops. And in time, Pops turned his life over to the Lord.

For twenty years, Pops was home every night at six to see his sweet bride. They went to the movies almost every weekend. And our family went to dinner with them almost every Wednesday night. Blake and Brooke would feed Kay and rush to be the first to push her in the wheelchair.

Sometimes our good health puts us at a serious disadvantage. We feel invincible. We feel we don't need God. But we do, of course, and Kay always helped me remember that. Whenever I thought I was having a bad day. I'd drop everything I was doing, get in my car, drive the fifty minutes to Santa Barbara to visit her. As soon as I walked into the room she would light up with a huge smile.

"Hi, Shelene!"

"Hi, Kay," I would say back, giving her a big kiss on the cheek. "How are you doing today?"

"Marvelous," she would say.

On December 31, 2013, Katherine Dickens went to be with the Lord. Pneumonia had taken its toll, and after twenty years of fighting her physical battle, Kay was ready to go home.

I will never forget what Francis Chan said about Kay at her funeral. "It was as if God allowed Kay to see what her true future would be. She had such a genuine smile and kindness toward everyone. It was as if, over those twenty years, God had let her see into heaven. See what was to come. How else can you explain being completely handicapped, with serious brain damage, and never complaining about anything, *ever*?"

There is no doubt in my mind that Kay saw her wonderful future from a distance, a future in which she is walking, running, and dancing once again. And God in His wisdom gave the gift of an extra twenty years to those of us who were privileged to be blessed by her smile, her selfless joy, and her unwavering, ridiculous faith.

Pops, Marian, and I were in the room with Kay when she took her last breath. When that moment came, I could only imagine what it must have been like for her to take her first breath in the presence of the Lord.

I am quite certain it was marvelous!

Lord, give me the perseverance to live for another world, a heavenly world. Help me to forsake bitterness and self-pity when life deals me difficult circumstances I do not understand. Grant me a sweet spirit not to complain about my circumstances but to look to the future, longing for the place You are preparing for me. And most of all, Lord, for the remaining years You have given to me here on earth, I pray You will empower me to live a life of great faith so that my life will be a shining light to others and bring a tenderhearted smile of joy to Your lips. Amen.

twenty-two

BACK TO THE BANK

More than twenty years had passed since the FBI investi-gators let me out the door of the Home Savings of America bank on Ventura Boulevard after the robbery. I never returned to that place. I was too afraid.

Until today.

The self-examination of my life while writing this book helped me recognize that I lived much of my early life in fear. I feared ever setting foot in that bank again, going to Africa without my husband, making a career change. I was afraid of surrendering my extreme comforts to God or of allowing my son to take a trip without me to India.

But fear is the opposite of faith, and God had been teaching me to live my life fearlessly, with full faith in Him. He had shown me so many examples of fearless faith. Noah did not fear the mockery of his community; Abraham obeyed God fearlessly, knowing his son would be spared. Moses "did not fear the wrath" of the pharaoh. Daniel was fearless in the face of vicious lions. The Watsons went forward fearless because of a message on a blanket. Francis did not fear the ex-felon living in his master bedroom.

Now God was pressing hard on my heart to go back to the

bank where I had been robbed at gunpoint more than twenty years before. I knew I didn't have anything in particular to fear about going back. But this was about turning yet another fear over to God.

So many changes had happened over the years that had passed. I had gone from being a newlywed to a new mom to a mom sending a child to college, from an intern to a business owner, an agent to a producer, a producer to running a charity with the goal of alleviating poverty. Even the bank name had changed from Home Savings of America to Washington Mutual and now to JPMorgan Chase.

But while the signs outside had changed, the building had always remained the same. I had passed this location hundreds of times in the twenty years that had passed, with the events of the robbery always running through my mind. This time it was different. This time I was stopping.

As I turned from Ventura Boulevard into the parking lot, I was shocked to see that the same spot where I had parked twenty years ago was open. I pulled in. I arrived at the same time as before, the lunch hour. I even brought a blue zippered bank bag with me. I knew there was no way the same thing was going to happen again, but I was still nervous. As I stepped through the same tall doors, a rush of air hit my face. The smell of the bank reminded me of my fear. I stepped in line holding my bank bag.

The bank wasn't as busy as it had been on that long-ago day. A clear, bulletproof Plexiglas barrier had been built from floor to ceiling in front of the teller counter I had once leaned against. I made sure to check out every single person in the bank. No one had a white T-shirt wrapped around his hand, concealing a weapon. There were only a few people ahead of me, but a line of busy people quickly started to form behind me.

Then I heard it.

Are you kidding me, Lord?

"Does anyone have a direct deposit?" the bank teller called out.

One, one thousand. Two, one thousand. Three, one thousand. Silence.

Okay, God, here it goes.

"I do."

As I said those words, just as I did twenty years earlier, I almost hit the floor, imagining someone was going to yell out, "Everyone down!" But I heard nothing except the sound of receipt printers and the hushed tones of people conducting bank business.

Then a promise I had memorized popped into my head: *Shelene, I will never leave you or forsake you.*

The teller motioned me to come to his Plexiglas window. As I walked up to the window with confidence and handed him my deposit, he smiled. We made a little small talk, and he gave me my receipt. Then I turned, gave the bank a triumphant look, and walked out to my SUV.

I sat in the front seat with a big smile on my face. I had come a long way. The firm commitment of an absurdly unbelievably good God had flooded my mind just when I needed Him the most. This visit was all about symbolism for me. It was a symbol of how I was choosing to absolutely trust Him, and how I knew He was absolutely trustworthy.

My fear had finally been replaced with faith. Solid faith. Ridiculous faith.

I'm not saying that the faith I had experienced in that split-second moment so many years ago was not real. It was intensely real, though it faded in time.

But my faith has grown so much stronger since then, through all the ways I've seen God move in my life and in the world. My faith is more seasoned, more confident, more trusting, more brave.

And much, much more ridiculous.

You can watch your faith grow like that too. Just take a step forward, even if you're afraid. Remember God's promises, lean on them, and take another step. God will take it from there, and the result will be absurdly, unbelievably good.

Look out, mountain. Here we come.

ACKNOWLEDGMENTS

Brice: **To the man I get to spend the rest of my life on** earth with. I love you and thank God for allowing me to be your wife. It's crazy to think we just celebrated our twenty-fifth wedding anniversary. This year we watched as our daughter got her driver's license and cried together as our son went off to college. This has been a ridiculous year that required ridiculous faith. Your godly, loving, faithful leadership has carried our family through the ups and downs life brings. Thank you for always reminding us to fix our eyes on things to come not on earthly things.

Blake: As I finish the final touches on this book you are finishing your first semester of college at Pepperdine University (#GoWaves). Although, you're not more than twenty miles away, every day I pass your quiet bedroom. I actually miss your dirty socks in the clothes hamper and Dad and I now have to take the trash cans down on Wednesday nights for pickup. This new season makes me realize this book about faith was written for me. For me to continue to have faith that God, not me, knows the plans He has for your life. I am honored to be your mom and pray that God will continue to bless the work of your hands for His glory.

Brooke: As I finish this book you are starting the second semester of your junior year of high school. You are growing into such a beautiful young woman after God's own heart. Besides being absolutely hilarious and making us laugh until we cry, your kind, loving, servant's heart blesses me more than you know. Your genuine love for people splashes over onto everyone around you. In this new season in our lives when you are the only child living at home, Dad and I look forward to quiet moments with you as well as loud cheering moments as we watch you on the lacrosse field and in the water-polo pool. Your hard-work ethic, love for learning, and dedication to doing your best as if doing it unto the Lord will take you far for His glory. Keep loving Him most.

The Weaver Family: To my little sister Shanda and my brother-in-love Greg and my two nieces Maddie and Saige. It makes me smile thinking about all the faith walks we've taken together, trusting God to guide the way. I love you all and feel blessed to call you family.

Pops: I love you with all my heart and thank God for placing you in my life twenty-two years ago. Adopting you was one of the best decisions I've ever made. I love our weekly Bible study lunches together. Watching you love and care for Kay until God released her back home with Him was one of the most selfless acts of Christ's love I've ever seen. You are a man of your word. You cared for Kay in sickness and in health. I am so glad I get to spend eternity with you both. Kay just got her mansion in heaven first. Let's keep investing in the "First National Bank of Heaven." As it has been said, He is no fool who gives what he cannot keep to gain what he cannot loose.

Barbara: Buddy!! What can I say . . . You have been my mentor since I was twenty-two. We have traveled the world together. Grown in our walks with the Lord. Shared the ups and downs, always knowing who was in complete control. Your loyalty, love, and friendship have blessed me more than words can say. Thank you for living a life of ridiculous faith.

Matt: You are a man of your word and the little brother I always wished I had. Thank you for always making time for your crazy sister's ideas. Whether we are producing, directing, building, serving, traveling, or just dreaming up ideas to change the world, your amazing talents and willingness to make a difference are *so* valued and appreciated.

Mark and Michelle Hiepler: Thank you for sharing your family with us. We love doing life with you. Your talents are endless, love for the Lord infectious, and your passion and work for something greater are respected. I've already asked God to make us neighbors in heaven so we can have GAMENIGHTS!

My Girlfriends/Sisters in Christ: Proverbs 27:6. I am beyond grateful to have each of you in my life. Barbara Cameron, Michelle Hiepler, Candace Cameron Bure, Lisa Chan, Karen Armstrong, Cheril Hendry, Karen Russell, Deb Lautner, Shannon McIntosh, Cindy Monroe, Kirsten Hayese, Leslie Bachman, Nina Davies, Laura Pettitte, and Kirstin Biegert.

My Tuesday morning BIBLE (not Babble) study girls: Thank you for diving into truth with me every Tuesday. I look forward to seeing each one of you every week.

Tammy and Eric Gustavson: Thank you for your awesome hospitality and particularly for letting us stay in your barn during the writing of many of these pages. The accommodations were a bit rough but I believe it brought out the best in me. Ha Ha ☺

My amazing assistant, Stacie Henry: You are a gift. Thank you for keeping me organized and for taking some of these crazy, ridiculous adventures with me.

My agents Rick Christian and Bryan Norman and the amazing team at Alive Communications: Thank you. I am honored to be a part of the family.

Chad and Julie Cannon: What can I say; I love you both with all my heart. Chad, thank you for believing in me to make this book happen. And thank you, Julie, for always opening up your home and allowing me to stay with y'all when I'm in from California. #grateful

The whole publishing team at Nelson Books: You are all amazing and I am forever thankful for all your gifts and talents. Janene, the most FABULOUS editor on the planet, Brian Hampton, Jeff James, Stephanie Tresner, Tiffany Sawyer, Mallory Collins, and Kristen Ingebretson.

The Skip1.org board and volunteers: Thank you for allowing me time to write this book. Thank you for loving the children we serve. Thank you for your consistent service and for showing up and living a life of ridiculous LOVE.

All my friends and family, you know who you are: Thank you for living a life of *Ridiculous Faith* with me. I love you and am forever honored to be in your life.

APPENDIX

God's Promises

- *I will never leave or forsake you.*
  "Be strong and courageous. Do not be afraid or terrified because of them, for the LORD your God goes with you; he will never leave you nor forsake you" (Deuteronomy 31:6).

- *I will pursue you with goodness and mercy.*
  Surely your goodness and love will follow me
    all the days of my life,
  and I will dwell in the house of the LORD
    forever.
  (Psalm 23:6)

- *I will show you how to live and keep watch over you.*
  I will instruct you and teach you in the way you should go;
    I will counsel you with my loving eye on you.
  (Psalm 32:8)

- *I will be with you and make you stronger.*
  So do not fear, for I am with you;
    do not be dismayed, for I am your God.

I will strengthen you and help you;
  I will uphold you with my righteous right hand.
(Isaiah 41:10)

- *I will renew your strength when you depend on Me. Your
  energy will not give out.*
  But those who hope in the LORD
      will renew their strength.
  They will soar on wings like eagles;
      they will run and not grow weary,
      they will walk and not be faint.
  (Isaiah 40:31)

- *If you stick close to Me, you will lead a fruitful life.*
  "I am the vine; you are the branches. If you remain in me
  and I in you, you will bear much fruit; apart from me you
  can do nothing. If you do not remain in me, you are like
  a branch that is thrown away and withers; such branches
  are picked up, thrown into the fire and burned. If you
  remain in me and my words remain in you, ask whatever
  you wish, and it will be done for you" (John 15:5–7).

- *I will give you words that you need to speak.*
  "For the Holy Spirit will teach you at that time what you
  should say" (Luke 12:12).

- *I will not let you be tempted beyond what you can bear.*
  "No temptation has overtaken you except what is com-
  mon to mankind. And God is faithful; he will not let you
  be tempted beyond what you can bear. But when you are

tempted, he will also provide a way out so that you can endure it" (1 Corinthians 10:13).

- *I will give you wisdom for every new challenge.*
  "If any of you lacks wisdom, you should ask God, who gives generously to all without finding fault, and it will be given to you" (James 1:5).

- *I will give you peace when you practice what I have taught you.*
  "Whatever you have learned or received or heard from me, or seen in me—put it into practice. And the God of peace will be with you" (Philippians 4:9).

- *I will take care of all your needs.*
  "And my God will meet all your needs according to the riches of his glory in Christ Jesus" (Philippians 4:19).

- *I will prepare a heavenly place for you so you can be with Me.*
  "My Father's house has many rooms; if that were not so, would I have told you that I am going there to prepare a place for you? And if I go and prepare a place for you, I will come back and take you to be with me that you also may be where I am" (John 14:2–3).

- *I will take good care of your future.*
  In their hearts humans plan their course,
      but the Lord establishes their steps.
  (Proverbs 16:9)

- *I am always there when you need Me.*
  God is our refuge and strength,
      an ever-present help in trouble.
  Therefore we will not fear, though the earth give way
      and the mountains fall into the heart of the sea,
  though its waters roar and foam
      and the mountains quake with their surging.
  (Psalm 46:1–3)

- *I will rescue you from your own faults.*
  "If you declare with your mouth, 'Jesus is Lord,' and believe in your heart that God raised him from the dead, you will be saved. For it is with your heart that you believe and are justified, and it is with your mouth that you profess your faith and are saved" (Romans 10: 9–10).

- *I will not allow anything to separate you from My love.*
  "For I am convinced that neither death nor life, neither angels nor demons, neither the present nor the future, nor any powers, neither height nor depth, nor anything else in all creation, will be able to separate us from the love of God that is in Christ Jesus our Lord" (Romans 8:38–39).

NOTES

RIDICULOUS? REALLY?

1. Dictionary.com Unabridged, s.v. ridiculous (Random House, n.d.), http://dictionary.reference.com/browse/ridiculous (accessed September 25, 2015).

CHAPTER 2: TO THE MOUNTAIN

1. Charles Haddon Spurgeon, "Sermon XIII: A View of God's Glory," *Sermons of Rev. C. H. Spurgeon of London, Second Series* (New York, Robert Carter & Brothers, 1883), 205.
2. I tell the story of how (and why!) Skip1 got started in my book *Love, Skip, Jump: Start Living the Adventure of Yes* (Nashville: Thomas Nelson, 2014). For more information about how you can get involved with Skip1, visit our website at www.skip1.org.

CHAPTER 6: COOLIO'S FAITH WALK

1. Anugrah Kumar, "Wallenda Constantly Prayed to Jesus During Successful Grand Canyon Tightrope Walk," Christian Post, June 14, 2013, www.christianpost.com/news/nik-wallenda -constantly-prayed-to-jesus-during-successful-grand-canyon -tightrope-walk-98616/ (accessed October 7, 2015).
2. Ibid.

CHAPTER 7: FREE TO GO

1. Charles Haddon Spurgeon, "Sermon III: The Snare of the

Fowler," *Sermons of Rev. C. H. Spurgeon of London, Third Series* (New York, Robert Carter & Brothers, 1883), 44.

CHAPTER 9: NATURALLY NOAH

1. R. C. Sproul, What Is Faith? Crucial Questions No. 8 (Lake Mary, FL: Reformation Trust, 2010), excerpted on Logos Bible Software sales page, https://www.logos.com/product/28070/what-is-faith.

CHAPTER 11: MESSAGE IN A BLANKET

1. John Piper, "What Faith Knows and Hopes For," *Desiring God*, June 1, 1997, http://www.desiringgod.org/messages/what-faith-knows-and-hopes-for (accessed October 7, 2015).

CHAPTER 15: CAN YOU SPELL THAT?

1. According to Wikipedia, cyclophosphamide is an International Nonproprietary Name (INN). Trade names for this drug include Endoxan, Cytoxan, Neosar, Procytox, and Revimmune. Also known as cytophosphane, this drug is a nitrogen mustard alkylating agent from the oxazaphosphorine group. See https://en.wikipedia.org/wiki/Cyclophosphamide.
2. Oxford Dictionaries, s.v. miracle, http://www.oxforddictionaries.com/us/definition/american_english/miracle?q=miracle.

CHAPTER 16: THE MASTER BEDROOM

1. Francis Chan, *Crazy Love: Overwhelmed By a Relentless God,* rev. and updated ed. (Colorado Springs, CO: David C. Cook, 2013).

ABOUT THE AUTHOR

Photo by Christa Foley

Shelene Bryan is the author of *Love, Skip, Jump* **and the** founder of Skip1.org, a charity dedicated to providing food and clean water to children in America and around the world. She lives in Southern California with her husband, Brice, and their two children.

Stay connected with Shelene and join her on some ridiculous adventures at Shelenebryan.com.

Twitter: twitter.com/shelenebryan
Instagram: www.instagram.com/shelenebryan
Facebook: www.facebook.com/shelenebryan
Periscope: www.periscope.tv/shelenebryan

skip1.org

skip something. feed a child.

Skip1.org is committed to bringing food and water to children and families in need. We do this by building new kitchens and renovating existing ones, financially supporting food distribution and feeding programs in places where kitchens can't be built and by supporting clean water and sustainable agricultural initiatives as needed.

Skip1.org currently has active projects in the Dominican Republic, Peru, Uganda, Rwanda, the Philippines, and North America.

Join Shelene Bryan, **Skip1.org**'s founder and author of *Love, Skip, Jump* in skipping something to help us feed children in need across the country and around the world.

9781400206162-A